Streetwalking
WITH JESUS

Streetwalking

WITH JESUS

Reaching Out in Justice and Mercy

John Green
with **Dawn Herzog Jewell**

Foreword by
Francis Cardinal George, O.M.I.

Illustrations by
Brian Bakke

Our Sunday Visitor Publishing Division
Our Sunday Visitor, Inc.
Huntington, Indiana 46750

Copyright © 2011 by John Green.

Published 2011

15 14 13 12 11 10   1 2 3 4 5 6 7 8 9

ISBN: 978-1-59276-930-8 (Inventory No. T1142)

LCCN: 2011924060

Cover design by Amanda Falk

Cover and interior images: Brian Bakke and Shutterstock

Interior design by Amanda Falk

PRINTED IN THE UNITED STATES OF AMERICA

Table of Contents

Endorsements

"*Streetwalking with Jesus* is one of the most intelligent and compelling calls to discipleship I've read in the past decade. Rooted in the experience of Chicago's Emmaus Ministries and Green's extraordinary outreach to male prostitutes — men often numbered among the most forgotten and despised of America's street people — this book is a vivid portrait of what real Christian witness looks like. It will leave you examining your own love of God and your own Christian faith with new eyes, and a new hunger to do more."

— Charles J. Chaput, O.F.M. Cap., Archbishop of Denver

"The work of Deacon John and Carolyn Green through Emmaus Ministries is the real deal, a living example of the love, persistence, patience, and grace of Christ poured out on the least of the least among us. Their passion, integrity and vision draws Christians of all stripes together to demonstrate in person the power of the Gospel, manifest both in word and deed in the lives of male prostitutes. This moving account of that work will bless and challenge readers to open our eyes to the broken brothers around us who need the stubborn love that John's ministry provides."

— Stanton L. Jones, Ph.D., Provost and Professor of Psychology, Wheaton College, Wheaton, Illinois

"Deacon John Green writes eloquently of grace and reconciliation on the streets of Chicago, thus revealing the dynamic power of the Spirit to transform hopeless lives. *Streetwalking with Jesus* introduces you to real ministry on the margins and shows how the power of shared vision actually works when Gospel ecumenism is rooted in our common witness to Jesus Christ."

— Dr. John H. Armstrong, President, ACT 3, author of *Your Church Is Too Small: Why Unity in Christ's Mission Is Vital to the Future of the Church*

"John Green weaves his journey with the narrative of Scripture and the narrative of lives lived on the street. The result is a threefold cord — a cord not easily broken — that tethers the compassion of God to the streets of Chicago. John sees the world of the marginalized through the eyes of God — that is to say he sees broken people and tragic things with the eyes of love. What he sees heals, convicts, and gives us all reason to think again about what it means to do justice, love mercy and walk humbly with God."

— Adele Calhoun, co-minister, Redeemer Community Church, Wellesley/Needham, Massachusetts, author of the *Spiritual Disciplines Handbook*

"Two thousand years ago, Jesus walked the streets ministering to the marginalized in society. John Green does the same with Emmaus Ministries. In this book, you will meet people who have been changed by John's loving heart, compassionate ears and pavement-pounded shoes. You will also discover one of the great lessons of ministry: 'one-on-one is how it's done.' This book brought me right back to the essentials of a Jesus-inspired lifestyle."

— Albert Haase, O.F.M., author of *This Sacred Moment: Becoming Holy Right Where You Are*

"John Green is a man whose heart beats with justice and mercy, and he certainly walks humbly with his God. He is a man with a vision to help the sexually broken, a segment of society that is largely ignored even by the church. As you read through the pages of *Streetwalking with Jesus*, you'll be challenged to think more deeply about your own faith journey, and certainly challenged to pray for the 'least of these.'"

— Anita Lustrea, Host & Executive Producer of Midday Connection-Moody Radio

"Having known John and his ministry firsthand for many years I can say that reading *Streetwalking with Jesus* brought back vivid memories, just as it will conjure up the imagination of those who have never met John in person. His descriptions of the spiritual journey that eventually led him to Uptown and of the people he has encountered in ministry make the reader feel as if he is streetwalking with John. More than that, the "Digging Deeper" sections at the end of each chapter do not allow the reader to walk away from the loving concern God has for hurting people and for his justice and mercy to prevail. John's book challenges us to engage in introspection about our own relationships with God and the people we encounter (or ignore) every day. If one has a heart that is breakable, the reader of John's book may just pocket his iPhone as he hurries off to the next meeting in order to see people on city streets through the eyes of Jesus."

—Dennis Okholm, Ph.D., Professor of Theology, Azusa Pacific University, Azusa, California, and author of *Monk Habits for Everyday People*

"John Green is the real deal. His words and lifestyle of compassion ooze from these pages. He and his team at Emmaus are modeling Micah 6:8 in this book and in their daily routine. The stories break our hearts. I have personally been deeply impacted on many Immersion Nights with Moody students. May your tribe increase, guys. You have left your mark on me."

— Dr. John Fuder, Professor of Urban Studies, Moody Theological Seminary, Chicago, Illinois

"If Jesus were incarnate on earth today where would he walk? To whom would he minister? With whom would he break bread? In *Streetwalking with Jesus*, John Green takes his readers on a journey that answers these questions. In so doing, he has written an instant 'classic' for all those yearning to follow the path of Christ. Green transports readers to the underbelly of modern urban life — to places littered with despair, addiction, poverty, and terrifying physical and sexual violence. He takes us on a journey to find lost sheep that have wandered, fallen or been cast to the outermost margins of society. He leads us through dark and dangerous streets to bring us face to face and heart to heart with men in prostitution — men society has largely forgotten, terribly vilified and horribly abused. Through the riveting real life accounts of more than twenty years of ministry to men who survive on Chicago's gritty streets by selling their bodies, Green puts flesh and bone on what it means to be the Body of Christ to those in need. Read this book at the risk of having your spirit shaken, of having your heart and soul rent with compassion for 'the least of these.' Read this book at the risk of learning that genuine Christian ministry isn't about keeping scorecards for Jesus, but about sharing the light and love of the Gospel one meal, one hug, one prayer, one hospital visit, one night of outreach at a time. Read this book at the risk of being called to make a living sacrifice of your life to the God who requires justice, mercy and humility."

> — **Lisa L. Thompson, Liaison for the Abolition of Sexual Trafficking, The Salvation Army National Headquarters, Washington, D.C.**

"The highest compliment that I can give to John Green's *Streetwalking with Jesus* is that it opens us to the very heart of God. As I read the stories of John's engagement with the broken lives on the streets of Chicago, I saw more deeply the compassionate heart of Jesus who both identifies with our brokenness and is outraged by the evil forces that create it. A crucial theme that runs throughout God's Word that we in the Christian community desperately need to embody is that our God is on the side of the discarded people of this world. John Green takes us to the streets where male prostitutes hang out, tells their stories, breaks our heart and compels us to action."

> — **Greg Ogden, Executive Pastor of Discipleship, Christ Church Oak Brook, Oak Brook, Illinois**

"Well all I can say is I laughed, I wept and punched my fist in the air with a big YES. An incredible down-to-earth story that will challenge your socks off. This book should be in the hands of anyone wanting to journey alongside those in prostitution."

> — **Josephine Wakeling, Ministry Leader and Advocate for Trafficking Victims, United Kingdom**

Foreword

Meeting and walking with male prostitutes might seem far from the road to Emmaus that Jesus walked after his resurrection (Lk 24:13-35). Those whom Jesus met didn't recognize him at first, and male prostitutes on the streets of Chicago often don't recognize him either. The miracle of God's grace lies in the fact that Emmaus ministers can see the face of Jesus when they look at and talk to the young men who prostitute themselves on the street and whose stories shape the narrative of this book.

Deacon John Green is part of that miracle. A man of deep faith, supported by his wife and family, John has taken the prophet Micah to heart. He walks the streets humbly, shows God's mercy to all and lives justly, in right relationship to all sinners because he knows the power of God's forgiveness in his own life (Mi 6:8). His work is rooted in his baptismal call to discipleship and strengthened by his ordination as a deacon of the Church, a servant who goes out to the poor in order to enrich them with the Gospel of Jesus Christ.

The greatest poverty is not to know Christ, and this conviction is why Emmaus Ministries will remain genuinely ministerial and not morph into a well-intentioned service group for young men who are down and out. Like most activities, as ministries develop they tend to become bureaucratic and sclerotic. John Green's story of how Emmaus Ministries first began and now continues shows how the scale of the work and the direct contact between those called to this ministry and those whom God has used to call them to it keep this ministerial activity literally close to the ground.

Working through the text and the questions posed at the end of each chapter will help the reader participate in this ministry, bringing it into his or her own vision of life. This book will help you see what you might have overlooked before. It will move you to ask yourself how to break out of the habits that too often take the place of happiness by imprisoning each of us in a routine that no one else, not even God, can break into. It will push you to ask about mission, about purpose in life and the way you spend your time. It's a good read and, more, it is a compelling narrative. If you take one step on the road to Emmaus, Christ will meet you on the way and the journeys of this book will become part of your path.

I am proud that John Green is a deacon of the Archdiocese of Chicago. I am grateful that he has written this book. I am confident that it will give all who read it and take it to heart new insight and more courage in our common quest to introduce Christ to male prostitutes and all others He died to save.

— Francis Cardinal George, O.M.I.
Archbishop of Chicago
November 1, 2010
The Feast of All Saints

Why I Wrote this Book

Ever since I was a young child, I've felt like a train on a set of railroad tracks. My job was to just chug along this well-worn line. Be a good kid. Get good grades. Go to the best college I could. Meet the nicest person I could. After that, get the best job I could. Move into the nicest and best neighborhood I could. Have a few good kids. And repeat. That was my mission: chug along and stay on the track.

After being raised like a good train and chugging along for a while, my faith in Christ caused me to start asking questions and taking steps off the tracks. It was uncomfortable at first, unfamiliar, and sometimes scary. But being willing to step off those tracks has opened me to a new life of mission.

For the last twenty years I've lived out that life and calling by reaching out to men involved in prostitution on the streets of Chicago. As my journey intersected with theirs, I learned new lessons of life and faith from them. I wrote this book because I want to challenge you, too, to step off those tracks.

Don't you wonder if there's something more? Something more than just being a train on the world's tracks?

I've found that "something more" through engagement with an Old Testament prophet's persistent questions and through a life among the poor. The something more is living a deeply intentional "missional" life.

Throughout this book I've tried to share stories and experiences from my journey that might help others in the Church make decisions and choices that would deepen their own sense of mission. While I've changed people's names and some biographical details to protect confidentiality, the stories tell the truth. I just don't want you to take them too literally. Use them as metaphors and mirrors. Although most of you probably don't hang out with male prostitutes, there are marginalized people all around you. Use what's here to reflect on how your own heart is oriented (or *not* oriented) to those in your world who are ostracized and overlooked.

But I hope it doesn't stop there. Little is gained by reading these stories if they don't expand your own heart's capacity for justice and mercy. My most fervent hope and prayer is that this book will break your heart. It's a painful process to be sure. But much is gained as well. That's why at the end of each chapter is a time for "Digging Deeper." The purpose of this section is to allow you some time for self-reflection and evaluation. Don't rush on to the next chapter. Stop. Listen. Reflect. Ask. Pray.

Two final suggestions. Keep a journal nearby as you read *Streetwalking*. Record your thoughts, reactions, and insights. Visit those pages again in a year or two and see what God has done. I also encourage you to read this book with other people. Jesus doesn't come to us by himself. He comes to us in community. We need our brothers and sisters on the journey of faith. Read this book with some others. Ask each other those questions at the end of each chapter and see where it leads.

Perhaps your journey will lead to laying some new tracks and going off in an unknown direction. Perhaps it'll be continuing on the path you are already on, but making the tracks your own and not the world's. However it happens, we have to step off the world's track. That's not our mission.

As those two famous and fictional Chicagoans Jake and Elwood Blues said in the movie *The Blues Brothers*, "We're on a mission from God."

You may also want to visit the books website: www. streetwalkingwithjesus.com. There you will find discussion forums related to the "Digging Deeper" sections, additional information on the artwork and music used in the book, related video and audio content, and upcoming web and in-person "Streetwalking" events.

Introduction

How John Green Became a Fool for Christ

I will never forget the sound of that suicide.

Falling from the top of the Port Authority Bus Terminal at the corner of Forty-second Street and Eighth Avenue in midtown Manhattan, his body must have been moving close to fifty miles per hour. The slap as he hit the unforgiving concrete pierced through the 2 a.m. clamor of Times Square.

People screamed.

A passing cop blew his whistle.

Sirens soon wailed in the distance.

I sat in a light blue outreach van at a light not more than ten feet from where he landed. My eyes caught the blur of his falling body just before I heard that sickening sound. I recognized him as a homeless man from the neighborhood. But I didn't know him. I didn't know his story. But I knew how it had ended: he had made his way to the top of the Port Authority Bus Terminal, stripped off all his clothes, and jumped.

Why?

I have no idea.

But it changed my life.

My story, at the time, was fairly succinct. All my life I had been the "good boy." I grew up in a good home in a wealthy neighborhood. I had good parents and a great family that instilled solid Midwestern, American values in me to the core. I was an altar boy at Mass. I was active in the parish youth group. I went to a Christian college. So why on earth was I driving an outreach van through the gritty streets of New York at two in the morning?

I had done many foolish things in my life, perhaps the most notable being an attempt at age nine to emulate Superman, which culminated in accidentally embedding a dart in my forehead. But going from the idyllic streets of Silver Lake Village near Akron, Ohio, to helping those ensnared in the sex trade in New York was a shift many others considered downright crazy.

The first inklings I had of doing something outside the parameters of "nice Christian" life arrived during my time at Wheaton College. My best friend in high school was Mike, an evangelical Protestant. We both shared our faith in Christ with our classmates. When we graduated in 1983, Mike decided to attend Wheaton College, a Protestant school outside of Chicago. If it was good enough for Mike, it was good enough for me. I applied and was accepted, little knowing that I would be one of twelve Roman Catholics in a student body of three thousand!

I arrived at Wheaton in the fall of 1983. Mike and I were roommates for our first three years. I was a member of the swim team and decided to major in Christian Education. My classes challenged me and the weekly chapel speakers were inspirational. But not a single day passed without someone asking me about my being Catholic. The questions ranged from the silly ("Why do you worship statues?") to the theological ("What about the difference between imputed versus infused righteousness?"). I did my best to respond to my classmates' questions, but often I didn't know the answer.

The constant questioning caused me to examine my Catholic faith. I read the documents of the Second Vatican Council, writings of the early Church Fathers, and papal encyclicals. As I learned the answers, my classmates' questioning taught me much about my Catholic faith.

Soon after arriving at Wheaton, I began attending St. Mark's, a local Catholic parish, and helping with the youth group a couple of nights a week. At the end of my freshman year, the husband and wife leading the youth group stepped down and I was hired as full-time youth minister. It was probably foolish to attempt full-time school and work, but I come from a long line of C-average students, so I didn't mind the hit my grades took.

One of the guest speakers who talked to that youth group changed the course of my life. Edwina Gateley was starting a ministry to women in prostitution in downtown Chicago. Both the kids and I were intrigued by her mission. Her passion for reaching these women was compelling. A few weeks later, a bunch of us piled into the church van to help her renovate an old house on Chicago's north side. I began driving to Genesis House on my own once a month to volunteer. I was handy, so I spent days repairing windows, fixing creaking hinges, or mending holes in the drywall. I attended Edwina's Bible studies and sometimes sat in the kitchen listening to volunteers who would talk with a woman prostitute — and sometimes her pimp. My eyes, ears, and heart were introduced to urban ministry.

Every so often, Edwina thanked me on my volunteer days by buying me lunch or dinner. Sometime in 1985, as we walked past the intersection of Addison and Halsted on the way to lunch, Edwina pointed out a group of men clustered at a street corner. She said, "Those guys over there are prostitutes, too. But nobody works with them; nobody cares about male prostitutes." And then we continued to lunch.

Male prostitutes? No way. "Why don't they just get a job?" was my first thought. It was hard for me to grasp the idea that guys would be out prostituting on the streets. I had no conceptual framework in my mind or heart for understanding what I was seeing. Yet, that brief image of a few guys standing on the bustling street corner, hustling themselves to the passing "johns" in cars, stuck with me.

About a year later, in February 1986, I was passing the forum board in the Wheaton College student union where students posted commentary about myriad issues. I noticed a *Reader's Digest* article about the work of Father Bruce Ritter and Covenant House in New York City. Here was someone reaching out to homeless and runaway kids, many in prostitution like the women and men I observed in Chicago. The end of the article included an invitation to join the Covenant House Faith Community by volunteering to work full time for a year with kids at the shelter. Three hours a day of prayer was required. Room and board, medical insurance, and a stipend of $12 a week was provided. When I finished reading, I knew I needed to go there. I don't know why or how I reached that conclusion; I just knew I had to go.

By the end of the spring semester of my junior year, I had applied and been accepted into the faith community, resigned my position as youth minister at St. Mark's, deferred my enrollment at Wheaton, sold my car, and then told my parents. They were not pleased. They believed the $36,000-plus that they had invested in my education was going down the drain.

I arrived in New York City in September 1986, a college dropout with a growing interest in reaching out to people on the streets, especially those involved in prostitution. Six months after I arrived in New York, I was working on the outreach program at night. We went in teams, driving a light blue van to neighborhoods where homeless kids gathered, and tried to bring them back to the shelter. We met hundreds of kids who were surviving on the streets. Some were petty thieves; some sold their blood and plasma at the blood bank; and hundreds of them, girls and boys, were selling their bodies. Along with these street kids, we met many other people of the "night community" — homeless folks, adult pimps and prostitutes, cops working the night shift, and "tricks" and "johns" out looking for a "date."

It was then that the homeless man jumped from the top of the Port Authority Bus Terminal. Wilfredo, my outreach partner, and I scrambled out of our van and ran to his body, but there was nothing we could do. We finished our overnight shift at 7 a.m., and I went to the chapel to pray with the faith community I was a part of. During the psalms and prayers, I couldn't get the sound of his body hitting the sidewalk out of my head.

After prayers, everyone else went up to breakfast. I made sure all the chapel doors were closed and then approached the cross. In front of our chapel stood a mural called "The Crucifixion on 8th Avenue," which depicted the story of Christ in a gritty, urban way. Jesus hung on the cross, one arm held up by a pimp, the other by a street kid who was piercing his side with a broken bottle. On both sides and under the cross were character scenes of the neighborhood: a cop on a horse talking into his radio, a young man handing out porno literature to commuters, an addict curled up on the sidewalk with drug needles around her, a pimp hustling some young kids, and many more.

I gazed at this mural and began to see street kids I couldn't reach: prostitutes I knew were out there, street people who were dying. I yelled at God. I demanded He do something about this mess. I cursed and cried and finally slumped into the front pew, spent and drained.

God was silent.

No visions, no voices of comfort, no feelings of peace — just the awesome silence of God. For a couple of days, I lived in a funk of despair and faithlessness. I felt abandoned. Then at morning prayer, on the third day, I listened to the words of the prophet Micah 6:8:

> He has showed you, O man, what is good.
> And what does the LORD require of you?
> To act justly
> and to love mercy

and to walk humbly with your God. (NIV)

The paradigm shifted. God spoke to me. I realized that all my life my values were based upon typical middle-class American values: hard work, doing good, living well, owning things, following the rules, and being the best that I could be. There is certainly some good in those things, but I heard God clearly say, "Those are not *my* values. I value justice, mercy, and humility. Those are *my* values."

From that day forward, I started asking three questions in my spiritual life: Lord, how can I live justly? To whom do I show mercy? And how may I walk humbly with you?

I stayed in New York for another year before returning to Wheaton College in January 1989 to finish my bachelor's degree and begin a master's program. It was then that I heard about a guy in Chicago named Mark Van Houten who was doing outreach to homeless people. I looked his number up in a Chicago phone book in the college library (Google had yet to be invented) and gave him a call. I told him I had just finished two years of street work in New York and would like to go out with him on the streets. He invited me to join him the following week.

On a Thursday night in September 1989, I met Rev. Mark at the corner of Wilson Avenue and Broadway in Chicago's Uptown neighborhood. About a mile north of Wrigley Field, along Chicago's beautiful lakefront, Uptown continues to be one of the most racially, culturally, and economically diverse communities in the country. Rev. Mark introduced me to Chicago street ministry. During my weekly outreach with him, we ran into a handful of guys prostituting in Uptown. I started trying to help them by buying them burgers and coffee from McDonald's or driving them to a shelter.

After a couple months with Mark, he set me loose on my own, and I focused on reaching out to men in prostitution. I knew I couldn't do this work by myself, so I asked for help from friends at Wheaton and my parish back in the suburbs. Some undergrads, a couple of professors, and former youth-ministry colleagues started driving down with me during the winter of 1989-1990. By the following summer, I was going out three nights a week, plus attending school full time and paying my bills by working nights at a local hospital as a "psychiatric technician" on a dual diagnosis, addictions, and mental health unit. The hospital work was great training for understanding the challenges that addicts with mental health issues face in their recovery.

In the summer of 1990, I headed to the Abbey of the Genesee, a Trappist Monastery outside of Rochester, New York. I needed a retreat — some peace and quiet to pray and discern what God wanted of me. It was five days of silence and solitude.

While I was at Covenant House in New York, I had discovered that long periods of contemplation gave me immense spiritual resources for street ministry. On the last day of this first retreat, I was walking around the small pond near the guesthouse. I felt the Lord say clearly that I should develop an outreach to men in prostitution, create a daytime drop-in center for them, and start a home where they could live.

I'm not one who has a direct line to the Almighty on a regular basis. In my spiritual life, I feel more like a drunk stumbling down an alley than a saint communing in a cathedral. I have felt I heard God speaking only two times in my life. The first was after reading that article on the college forum board in 1986. This was the second.

God's direction was clear, but, unfortunately, He was not very specific on the details of how long this would take. In the fall of 1990, the handful of volunteers and I decided to organize our work. Inspired by the post-resurrection story of Jesus walking with the disciples on the road to Emmaus (Lk 24:13-35), we called our fledgling mission Emmaus Ministries.

We went to work. We arranged for three nights a week of regular outreach. We sent letters to friends and family asking for support. Upon Rev. Mark's advice, I signed up with an organization called MidAmerica Leadership Foundation[1], under the direction of Rev. Bud Ipema. Bud helped me gather trusted leaders to form a board of directors for this new thing called Emmaus Ministries. Over the next two years, through this partnership, our fledgling idea grew into a concrete and thriving ministry.

I remember clearly one of our first board meetings in early 1991. I had been asked by one of the board members to draft an initial vision and plan for this outreach to men involved in prostitution. I came to the meeting with a single 8½ X 11 inch sheet of paper showing an array of staff, outreach centers, and homes that I expected to create for these men. My timeline for accomplishing everything was about eighteen months.

One of the board members, Chris Ellerman, asked if I had shown this to anyone else. I said, "No." He said, "Good." Then he crumpled the paper in front of me.

"John," he said, "this is going to be a very hard ministry to get off the ground. It's not something most people in the church, let alone in society, know about, let alone care enough to donate to. This work will not be built in a year or even two. If you are not in this for the long haul, for at least the next five to ten years, then we are all wasting our time."

Almost ten years later, we had developed a solid outreach ministry, a drop-in center and a residence called "Emmaus House." I laughed to myself when we first opened the house, recalling that board meeting and crumpled plan; it really did take that long.

Some would say that launching a ministry to prostituting men was folly. "Nobody cares about them." But as we celebrate twenty years of ministry, despite all the ups and downs I thank God for calling me and many others to such foolishness.

The sections of this book follow the questions from Micah, starting with "What does the Lord require of you?" This is not a memoir or a how-to book on starting an urban ministry for prostituting men. This is simply a series of reflections on these questions. The asking of these questions has led me into a life of ministry among men whom our society deems worthless. It has been a transformative process and journey for me. I believe that by asking these questions, our hearts and souls can be transformed, and our lives more deeply reflect that missional living the Gospels call us to.

For me, this story began at that intersection of 42nd Street and 8th Avenue in New York City with the tragic ending of the life of someone I will never know. I've come to many other intersections since then, asphalt and spiritual. Some are tragic, some filled with joy, some easy to cross, and some calling for a change in direction.

God works in us, and on our stories, at these intersections. They are moments of grace and challenge. They are moments when our stories change, deepen, and grow. Through the intersections in my journey, God has guided me into a life I could never have imagined.

Section I

What Does God Require of Me?

He has showed you, O man, what is good.
And what does the LORD require of you?
To act justly
and to love mercy
and to walk humbly with your God.

— Micah 6:8, NIV

All of us, poor and rich alike, have been conditioned by our upbringing. Impoverished men and women may become lulled into a state of "learned helplessness," without hope to change their lives. Likewise, the wealthy can walk in a state of "learned blindness," ignoring the desperation of the local and global poor.

What does God require of you and me?

Only this — to break out of our conditioning. If we do so, living justly will mean being willing to step into the lives of our brothers and sisters. Showing mercy will be painful but joy-filled. Walking humbly with God will entail serving as an agent of grace by guiding others out of the cage of learned helplessness, even in the moment of death.

Chapter 1

Learned Helplessness

In the early 1970s, researchers at a Pennsylvania university studied how dogs could be conditioned to a state of "learned helplessness." It sounds complicated, but it was simple. In a process now justly considered inhumane, the researchers closed a dog in a metal cage and sent electric shocks into the animal. At first, the dog reacted quickly, frantically running around, trying to get out. The researchers observed that as the shocks continued, it reacted less and less. Finally, the dog reached a point where it hardly moved as it was being shocked. The researchers then opened the door to the cage, offering the animal a clear exit, and continued the shocks. But the dog had reached the state of "learned helplessness." It lay there, enduring the shocks. Next, the researchers placed an unconditioned dog in the cage with the conditioned animal. When the treatments resumed, the new dog reacted and ran out of the cage. The conditioned dog observed this, got up, and ran out also.[2]

What a great metaphor this is for the Christian missional life!

My first reaction to seeing a group of men prostituting themselves was to ask, "Why don't they just get a job?" It was only after several years of walking with these men and listening to their stories that I realized that it wasn't that easy. They were conditioned. If I wanted to help, I would need to get in their cage.

One young man who taught me this was Jim.

* * * *

The Illinois State's Attorney looked into the jury box while his outstretched hand pointed behind him to the defense table.

"Jim *Jacobs* or Jim *Jacobson*," the lawyer shouted. "What does it matter? Who cares? He's just a *hustler*. He's just a *prostitute*! Who knows what his *real* name is?"

With that, he closed his final argument. Even though the attorney didn't say it outright, his message was clear: The man accused of murder didn't matter because he was a prostitute. Because he was a prostitute, he was of no worth to society. Because he was of no worth to society, he should not be trusted, or given rights, or believed when he testified that "I didn't do it."

Let me fill in the pieces for you.

About two years before that court scene in the late 1990s, I was talking with Jim in the corner of our ministry center's basement living room. A man in his early 30s, Jim sat with his coat pulled around him, his small build swallowed up by his jacket. His curly blond hair was as messy and dirty as his jeans and shirt. I knew by looking at him that he was sleeping in alleys and parks, even with the Chicago winter approaching. Around us, other guys were coming and going. Dishes from lunch clattered their way into the dishwasher. A rhythm-and-blues tune played on the radio. Jim spoke softly.

"I got tested last week," he said. "I'm positive. The doctor said my viral load was low, which is good. I can't believe this is happening."

I'd known Jim for a while. He had been slowly coming to grips with his life on the street and making changes in the right direction. For weeks he had felt ill, but he didn't want to visit the doctor for fear of learning he had

HIV. His fears had come true.

"I've gotta do right now, John," he continued. "I don't want to die. I called those people at Teen Challenge that you told me about. They said they got an HIV floor that I could stay on. I'm gonna go down for the interview tomorrow."

I listened as Jim talked, and I said a quiet prayer. Too often it's something like this that finally wakes a guy up to changing his life. I was sorry for him, but glad he was finally coming around.

A couple weeks went by before Jim came by again. He looked great. A new haircut, nice clothes, and clean face did him wonders. Even so, since I knew he hadn't gone to Teen Challenge's drug rehab program, I feared for him.

"I'm staying with a friend," he said, and my heart sank. Often when our guys say that, they mean they are staying with one of their "tricks" or "dates" — sometimes called "sugar daddies" — who generally are older men. As they get to know each other, the sugar daddy may begin to let the hustler stay with him occasionally. The sugar daddy provides a warm place to stay, food, clothes, and whatever else a hustler may want, in return for sex on demand.

It is an awful situation. These twisted relationships often entail real needs that the two men are trying to meet. The sugar daddy has a nurturing, parental need to give; and the hustler craves to be loved. When you're living day by day on the streets, a twisted love is sometimes better than no love at all.

"He's not asking me to do anything," Jim argued when I confronted him about his living situation. I didn't believe him and told him so. He said he knew what he was doing and that he didn't want to live on the streets while waiting to get into a residential rehab program like Teen Challenge.

A couple of weeks passed and Jim seemed to be gaining some weight and doing his best to stay clean. One Wednesday evening he came by for dinner and stayed for the prayer and worship time afterward. Jim thanked us for the evening and headed out the door for "home."

Two days later he called me on the phone.

"John, you gotta believe me, I didn't do this!" He was frightened. His voice cracked and wavered between fear and anger.

"They had me in a little room for hours. I thought they were going to kill me. I signed the confession because they told me to. I didn't kill him!"

Jim told me his side of the story. After leaving our ministry center, he went home. His sugar daddy wanted to have sex with him but Jim didn't, so he left. Jim admitted to me that he went out and got high and drunk. He came home around 3:00 a.m., opened the door, and found the sugar daddy dead on the floor, strangled. Jim called the police. The police questioned him for twenty-one hours and said he confessed to the murder. Jim said he was threatened into signing the confession.

The next day I visited Jim in Cook County Jail. Behind the two-inch-thick Plexiglas, I saw him enter wearing the tan inmate jumpsuit. Thankfully, I was the only visitor there at the time and the room was quiet. "Thanks for visiting me, John," he said. "I don't know what I'm going to do. You gotta believe me. I did not do this."

I asked him about his health. The county jail is probably one of the worst places to get good health care, especially for someone who's HIV positive. Jim said he was feeling fine. Then his face dropped and his eyes began to well with tears.

"If I had just done what you said I wouldn't be here. I swear if I get out of this, I'll get my life together. I'll go to Teen Challenge; I'll go wherever I gotta to get straight. If I'd just . . . "

Jim and I talked more. I encouraged him to get involved with the prison ministries. We talked about how faith in Jesus is not hindered by Plexiglas windows or prison walls. Jim said he was already getting to know Christian inmates. We prayed until the guard told us visiting time was over.

Why would any person in his right mind sign a confession to a murder he did not commit?

I have to admit that's the first question that ran through my head. I didn't know if Jim was telling the truth. But his signed confession was strong evidence against him. Regardless of his guilt or innocence, I knew we were the only people in his corner.

I made a few calls. After a couple of days one of the top three law firms in Chicago agreed to take his case. One of the partners is a godly man who is active in urban ministry in our city. He persuaded his firm to take up the challenge of Jim's case.

Jim sat waiting behind bars for about eighteen months while his attorneys gathered evidence, gave him a battery of tests, and hired a private detective to follow leads. My staff and I kept visiting Jim, volunteers wrote him, and many people began to pray for him. As many guys do, Jim began to get serious about his walk with Jesus while in prison. I'm not sure exactly when, but he opened himself to praying and reading his Bible. It was a blessing to see. But overshadowing that was the forty to sixty years in prison he was facing.

As the trial loomed closer, the state offered Jim a plea bargain: take a sentence of twenty years and he would be out in ten. If the case went to trial and the state won, it would push for the maximum sentence of sixty years.

The evidence the state had to bargain with was the signed confession. That's it. Absolutely no other evidence that Jim had committed the murder.

Jim was resolute. He wanted to go to trial because he was not guilty.

As the trial began, Jim's attorneys brought forth their evidence. The night of the murder Jim was not even at the sugar daddy's home. He was at another trick's apartment getting high. A few months earlier, the Chicago Transit Authority — which runs the public buses — switched from a coin-like token system of payment to a transit card system. The transit card is like a credit card with a magnetic strip on the back. Besides storing the amount of money available in your account, the strip also shows where you've been! When the police arrested Jim, the transit card he carried backed up his claim that he'd been at the other end of the city at the time the murder took place.

The defense attorneys brought in doctors to testify about Jim's mental state. They explained that Jim had been born with fetal alcohol syndrome, which severely affected his learning ability and comprehension. As a child, Jim was beaten with a baseball bat by his mother's boyfriend, causing acute brain damage. This physical abuse hindered his short-term memory and limited his ability to perform simple tasks like setting an alarm clock. These conditions made it hard for him to get and keep a job. For the last decade, Jim had lived on the streets, abusing drugs and prostituting to get by.

Hustlers like Jim don't prostitute because they enjoy it. It's a means of survival and what appears a choice to us is based on severely limited options. These guys "usually have low levels of formal education and their work choices are limited to unskilled labor which pays them much less that the 'easy money' provided by sex work."[3]

The doctors testified that, due to his brain damage and life on the streets, Jim's ability to comprehend what was happening to him during those twenty-one hours of interrogation at the police station was very limited. In addition, the police did not follow up on a host of other clues in the apartment where the sugar daddy was found. A third person's fingerprints, a beer bottle in his car, eyewitness accounts of other men in the apartment, and other evidence were ignored because the police had secured a signed confession.

At the trial, the police officer who had read Jim his confession painstakingly told the jurors that there was no way Jim could have misunderstood what he was signing. The officers had made every effort to "do it by the book." The eight-page confession had been read to Jim and witnessed by other officers. The officer testified that Jim had not been coerced or misled into signing the confession.

And yet, as the defense attorney pointed out, the police officer who had read Jim his confession and was so concerned with getting everything right didn't realize that she was mispronouncing his name the whole time. The confession read "Jim Jacobs," not "Jim Jacobson."

The trial took a week. An Emmaus staff member came every day to support and encourage Jim.

The jury returned its verdict in less than four hours: not guilty.

Jim was released twelve hours later. He stayed with my wife, Carolyn, and me in our apartment's guest room for a couple of weeks before moving into a home for homeless people in our neighborhood.

＊＊＊＊

It's distressing how our society views guys like Jim as disposable. "Who cares?" the State's Attorney had thundered. "He's just a prostitute!"

I care.

The Lord cares.

I trust you care, or you probably wouldn't be reading this book.

Anyone who wears the mantle of Christ should care what happens to these guys.

The cage of poverty, neglect, physical abuse, and trauma often steer guys like Jim into a state of "learned helplessness." In part because of their conditioning, it's not that easy to "just get a job." Understanding where they've come from and hearing their stories is messy and painful — it's like stepping into their cage. Yet, I learned stepping inside was crucial in order for me to understand who these guys were. And stepping inside was essential to begin answering the question: "What does the Lord require of you?"

Digging Deeper

Listen and Reflect

"Part of the Fabric Here" can be listened to at www.greenchoby.com/music-39.html. My wife, Carolyn, is a singer/songwriter. She and her music partner, Mike Choby, have been performing original acoustic music together since 1996. Many of Carolyn's songs speak to our life and ministry at Emmaus. She wrote this song when Jim lived with us for a few weeks.

Read and Reflect

When I look at your heavens, the work of your fingers,
the moon and the stars that you have established;
what are human beings that you are mindful of them,
mortals that you care for them?
Yet you have made them a little lower than God,
and crowned them with glory and honor.

— Psalm 8:3-5

For Discussion

As the Roman Catholic Archbishop of Olinda and Recife, Brazil, Dom Hélder Pessoa Câmara witnessed many lifetimes' worth of suffering, homelessness, poverty, and injustice. He died at the age of ninety on August 27, 1999. At one point in his ministry, he said, "If I give food to the poor and hungry, they call me a saint, but if I ask why the poor are hungry, they call me a communist!"

1. What do you find alarming in this chapter?

2. Is it hard to see someone like Jim as clothed with glory and honor?

3. What about the sugar daddy who was murdered?

4. What is the danger in asking what causes a man to get into a life of prostitution?

Pray

"Dear God in Heaven, for all children who have been abused and neglected, have mercy on them, Lord. Help those of us who have eyes to see and ears to hear to not turn from them when there is a need to intervene or speak up on their behalf."

Chapter 2

Learned Blindness

Imagine . . .

A nation is in turmoil. Political, religious, and economic fault lines divide the country. The gap between the rich and poor continues to grow. Politicians distort the truth to build their own power-base. The comfortable and powerful feel at ease while the powerless are hungry. Compared to their neighbors, these people have unprecedented prosperity and political stability, yet the threat of war and terror looms in the distance.

This description of the nation of Israel in the seventh century B.C. sounds much like our own.

Into this turmoil entered a young farmer boy named Micah, whom God called to go and preach to the wealthy and powerful of his day. Micah's message was clear: unless you repent and change how you treat the poor and the alien, bad things are going to happen.

Israel wouldn't/couldn't hear, and the Assyrian army came knocking.

Why didn't they hear? What clouded their vision and hardened their hearts?

John Shorack, a missionary with InnerCHANGE, writes:

> According to Amos, a prophet of the same era [as Micah] that preached in the north, the comfortable, power-holding class of people felt "at ease in Zion" and "secure on the mount of Samaria" (Amos 6:1-8). The disparity between rich and poor, between the powerful and the powerless, was growing perhaps more than at any time in Israel's history. The wealthy felt no tinge of conscience about the inner ruin of society and no foreboding of the deluge that was about to come. [4]

Could all the good people of Israel have intentionally grown calloused to the needs of the poor?

Probably not. In fact, Micah 6:6 asks, "With what shall I come before the Lord?" (NIV). God's people were willing to act, but they didn't have a clue how they got where they were.

Why?

Because they were conditioned.

As I became friends with guys involved in prostitution, I realized that I had also been conditioned. The wealth, comfort, security, and privilege I had grown up with were just as powerful conditioning factors as the poverty, neglect, abuse, and deprivation that guys at Emmaus experience. The only difference is that the poor can be conditioned to a state of "learned helplessness," while I was being conditioned to a state of "learned blindness."

— When I was a boy coming home from school in the 1970s, a creaky sound and smoky smell hit me first as I entered my house. The rhythmic "creak, creak" of my grandfather's rocking chair grew louder as I climbed the stairs. I turned left at the top to head to his room. He would be puffing on his pipe, rocking in his chair, and always ready to sneak me a piece of candy. I had the privilege of knowing a loving grandfather and other healthy men.

— I lived my boyhood in a safe neighborhood where I played with other kids from solid families. My mom has no idea how many times my buddy Mike and I almost fell out of that pine tree and died. It was two houses down from ours and rose into the sky like Jack's beanstalk. Mike and I spent at least a half-hour at a time winding up through the branches; our climbing disturbed pine cones that dropped to the ground far below. As the top swayed slightly in the wind, we took in the view that stretched for miles. It seemed like you could see forever.

— During the 1980s at Wheaton College, my favorite place to study was on the immaculate front lawn with my back against a tree and my books scattered around me. I would watch students playing with Frisbees or squirrels hunting for nuts in nearby bushes until, eventually, I remembered to study again.

— In the 1990s, access to wealth led Carolyn and me to the dilapidated brick building at 921 W. Wilson Avenue in Chicago. Drug dealers had operated here. Inside doors hung off their hinges, windows were cracked, and the second floor stunk to high heaven. Many people, up to no good, had hung out on the front and back porches. I thought the place was perfect — perfect for our ministry and a place to call home. We had enough saved for the down payment but not for the rehab this six-unit apartment building needed. A call to Mom and Dad in Silver Lake got us half of what we lacked. Then we put the remaining $50,000 on credit cards!

What do these four snippets of my life have to do with anything? In each of them are the seeds of blindness. If not for men like Fred, I could have remained blind my whole life.

* * * *

About a year after one of our outreach teams met Fred on Halsted Street, he came by our ministry center. Our drop-in center is a place of hospitality, prayer, and discipleship. Its comfortable atmosphere and caring staff and volunteers are a respite from the streets. Fred was a mess when he first arrived. Hanging out on the streets, sleeping with other men on the weekends, and drinking himself into oblivion had taken its toll.

Slowly, with much pain, struggle, and determination, Fred started becoming a new person. But it wasn't easy.

One day he and I were working in the back parking lot of our Emmaus building, priming the neighboring garage wall that faces our building. We had received permission to paint a mural on that side. Fred, some other guys, and a summer arts camp from a local church were going to paint a mural of a modern-day prodigal son. We have a lot of murals at Emmaus. Many of our guys are barely literate. Handing them a Bible or a nice, shiny brochure doesn't do much. But a twelve-by-sixty-foot mural of the prodigal son story can tell them a lot.

But before the artwork could go up, we had to properly prepare the wall's surface. Fred stood on a ladder, white primer splattering his clothes.

"I don't know wha'chor problem is!" he shouted angrily from his perch.

A fellow named Manny was looking up from the parking lot and trying to get Fred to leave with him.

"Well, I'm leavin'. With or without you!" Manny yelled as he stomped away.

At first, it might have seemed that two friends were having a spat. But I knew differently. Fred and Manny were in a sexual relationship, and Fred had been trying to end it.

"I don't know what to do, John," he said to me. "The more I've prayed and talked with Sill [our ministry director] the more I realize this isn't what I want. I've always known that the reason I slept with men was 'cause when I was a kid my father raped me."

Fred stopped and then went back to painting, frustration and tears welling up in his eyes. I didn't push. I'd heard his story before. His father physically and sexually abused him as a young boy and eventually abandoned the family. Unfortunately, this kind of abuse is so rampant in our country that the Centers for Disease Control (CDC) estimates that one in six boys are sexually abused before the age of eighteen.[5]

As Fred entered his teen years, still yearning for male affirmation, his athletic frame caught the attention of a male neighbor who seduced him. This was the start of a series of gay lovers and a search for fatherly love that eventually led to prostitution. In the midst of that, Fred got married to a woman and had two kids.

His confusion is typical of guys who prostitute. In a large study of male hustlers in New York City, almost three-quarters of the men self-identified as heterosexual or bisexual and reported both male and female sexual partners.[6]

That's a hard reality for most people to understand. Usually people assume all men who prostitute themselves are gay. That's not the case. Most are heterosexuals who are engaging in survival sex as a means to get by. Not only is all this sexually confusing to guys like Fred, but the prevailing, politically correct view of sexuality in our culture doesn't help either.

Three major myths about homosexuality are woven into our culture's conventional wisdom. The first is that people are born gay. The second is that you can go from being heterosexual to homosexual but not the other way around. The third is if you try to change your homosexual feelings, you'll do great harm to yourself. None of these is true. Unfortunately, men like Fred get caught in the midst of this cultural confusion.[7]

Back on that day at the mural, I tried to think of what to say to Fred, how to encourage him, when he stopped again and turned to me.

"You guys have been great friends to me." Then he fell silent and continued painting.

Like all of us, Fred has good days and bad days. Days when he is walking close to the Lord, other days when he seems to be running in the opposite direction. But by the grace of God, Fred was making it; he was turning his life around, one step and one decision at a time.

Not long after our day of painting, I shook Fred's hand and welcomed him into our Emmaus House Residence. The house first opened in 1999, but is closed now due to lack of funding. When Fred first arrived, it was an apartment in our building where six to eight of our guys could live and work on getting their lives back together. As we welcomed Fred, the excitement on his face was evident to everyone.

Despite the good changes in Fred's life, the first month in the Emmaus House Residence was hard for him. He hadn't found a job and continued to struggle with staying clean and sober, relapsing once and getting drunk. At the drug assessment we sent him to after his relapse, he was told to begin intensive outpatient treatment for alcoholism at a local clinic. He stormed out of the session and came home angry. He wanted to pack up and leave, to return to the streets where he knew how to survive and wouldn't have "anybody in my business." After a night of talking with our staff, he called the program, apologized, and signed up for the outpatient treatment.

* * * *

I thank God for Fred.

Knowing him has helped keep me from becoming blind. Our two lives couldn't have been more different.

Fred had an abusive father who called him "faggot" and "queer" growing up. I had a kindly grandfather who smoked cigars, played a mean game of rummy, and snuck me candies when my mom and dad weren't looking.

Fred's childhood playground was a tenement on Chicago's south side. He could have died from stray gunshots that echoed weekly around his home. I climbed trees and dodged falling pine cones.

Fred got an education in sexual exploitation as he gave his body to man after man, seeking an elusive love that would not abandon him. I got a BA in Christian Education at a private college that cost my parents tens of thousands of dollars.

Fred hasn't had a home in fifteen years. He has no family to speak of and can't find a job. I own a six-unit apartment building that used to be a crack house but now is a community of urban ministry. I have an awesome family: three sons, a daughter, and a wife who agreed to a crazy life of ministry to men involved in prostitution!

The degree to which I am blessed staggers me.

The degree to which I take that for granted shames me.

I've come to see how the American consumer culture tries to tell me that my life is comprised of rights. It is my birth-right as an educated, white, middle-class male to have a good job, be a success, own stuff, have an education, be secure, blah, blah, blah . . .

I think that's a load of crap.

It's all gift, all blessing. It's all from God, not from man. And it's to God, not to man, that I'm responsible for what I do with that blessing. I thank God for people like Fred who remind me not only of the blessing, but also the responsibility that follows.

How easily I could have fallen into a state of "learned blindness" to that responsibility. Jesus once remarked that "the poor will always be with you." I think He said this because we who are rich need the poor to keep us from becoming blind.

Digging Deeper

Listen and Reflect

"What My Living Has Brought" is available at www.greenchoby.com/music-40.html. After some intense dreams, Carolyn wrote this song as a reflection on how she would end up looking back at her life.

Read and Reflect

Leviticus 19:9-15 gives a glimpse of God's desire for our lives, including this verse: "You shall not render an unjust judgment; you shall not be partial to the poor or defer to the great: with justice you shall judge your neighbor" (19:15).

For Discussion

The book *Beyond Gay*, by David Morrison, is one of the best I've read on issues of sexuality and our contemporary culture. Archbishop Charles J. Chaput,[8] a Franciscan friar and the Roman Catholic Archbishop of Denver, writes the following in the foreword to this book:

> Leon Bloy, the French Catholic writer and convert from Judaism, once said, "Man has places in his heart which do not yet exist, and into them enters suffering, in order that they may have existence." It's one of my favorite quotations. Just about all of Christian scholarship on the nature of suffering can be reduced to these few simple words. Suffering can bend and break us. But it can also break us open to become the persons God intended us to be. It depends on what we do with the pain. If we offer it back to God, He will use it to do great things in us and through us, because suffering is fertile, it can grow new life.

1. How do you relate to feeling immensely blessed?

2. How does being "the persons God intended us to be" conflict with our contemporary culture?

3. Do you agree or disagree with the "three myths" about homosexuality that I mention above? If so why, or why not?

Pray

"Father in Heaven, we lift up all those young boys sexually abused by their earthly fathers, brothers, uncles, and neighbors. May they find healing for their 'father-wound' in a deep and personal relationship with You."

Chapter 3

My parents abandoned me when I was nine years old.

Not on purpose, though. On a family road-trip vacation to Florida, we must have stopped at a dozen antique stores between the Ohio state line and Disney World. My folks were "antiquers" and loved nothing more than spending an hour browsing through old stuff at some out-of-the-way shop. One afternoon in a small town in Georgia, they pulled up to yet another place. I was sleeping in the back of our brown, Buick station wagon under a pile of blankets. They left the windows down and went into the store.

I woke up a little later, noticed the antique store, and groaned. It was taking forever to get to Disney World! I got out of the car, saw a comic-book store next door, entered, and started perusing the shelves for Spiderman and my other favorite superheroes. Meanwhile, my folks returned to the car, saw the pile of blankets in the back and drove off, thinking I was still asleep.

Sometime later I came out of the store and found that my parents were gone. A jolt of fear and panic shot through me and I started to cry. The kindly antique-store owner came out and assured me my folks would return soon. The comic-book-store owner came out, put his hand on my shoulder, and said, "Don't worry, son, they'll be back." Then he handed me a few free comic books to read while I waited. A small crowd of kind, good-natured folks gathered and tried to console this stranded young boy. Somebody even bought me a chocolate shake from a nearby ice cream stand.

Their presence and kindness didn't take away my fear, but it gave me courage.

About a half-hour later my folks' Buick came roaring up to the store, brakes squealing as it skidded to a stop, and my relieved parents jumped out. I rode the rest of the day in the front seat reading comic books and slurping my shake while it lasted.

I still remember that first jolt of fear. But I also remember the courage I found in the actions and words of strangers willing to help.

Actress and author Dorothy Bernard once said, "Courage is fear that has said its prayers." As I worked with young men at Emmaus, I learned that I couldn't expel their fear by stepping into their cages, but I could help them find courage.

If you want to understand the young men with whom we journey, you have to understand fear, because it's their constant companion.

Have you ever stopped to think what your life would be like if you were always afraid? Much of our efforts in life revolve around reducing fears. We fear for our children's futures, so we send them to the best schools we can. We fear for our family's safety, so we spend hundreds a year on a home security system. We fear disaster, so we meet with our insurance agents and buy health, disability, home, car, life, and sometimes even "umbrella" insurance to cover just about anything. And when the day is done, we rest in the comfort of knowing we've done our best.

But what if, like our guys, you *didn't* rest comfortably and felt no comfort during the day? What if you slept fitfully, fearful of someone stealing your shoes while you dozed? What if, while seeking work in a department store, you feared the dreaded question, "Will you fill out this application, please?" because you didn't know how to read or write? What if you were afraid just walking down the street as your mind raced with each new sound? (A car accelerates suddenly behind you; could it be a gang drive-by? Someone trying to sell you drugs calls out "You straight?" and you cringe, hoping you can pass by them without an incident. A police squad car rolls by slowly and you fear the officers will stop you.)

Most of our guys have two coping mechanisms. One is hyper-passive aggressiveness and the other is violence. Harvey demonstrated both of these well while he, three other guys, and I were in the north woods of Wisconsin at HoneyRock Camp for a week.

* * * *

I kept my eyes fixed on the snow and gravel that crunched beneath my boots. My feet were carrying me to one of those situations where I didn't have a clue what to do. Moments before, Harvey and Shelton had gotten into a fistfight that had ended quickly after Harvey lifted Shelton into the air and slammed his body onto the ground. That's when I started moving, and by the time I got there Harvey had Shelton pinned to the ground, his knee pressing mercilessly into Shelton's neck.

"Whadaya say now, you *&%#?" Harvey growled. "Where's your mouth now!"

I pushed Harvey off Shelton and put my hand firmly on Harvey's shoulder.

"Come on, Harvey. Walk with me."

Separating the two of them seemed like a good idea right then, and so I took Harvey around a building to talk. He told me something about Shelton mouthing off to him, and although I had seen and heard that happen, I knew it wasn't the cause. I also knew I needed to de-escalate the situation because we had a morning's worth of work to do for the camp and needed to get started.

After I talked to each of them alone, the two combatants came to a semi-truce and we headed off to work. A verbal sparring match a few minutes later helped me decide to send the two on separate work details. Shelton left to help clean the dining hall's restrooms. Harvey, the others, and I walked to the rear of the camp to cut firewood.

But even with Shelton gone, Harvey was still filled with pent-up rage. He soon stopped chopping wood and began yelling at me.

"Why'd ya get me on those *&%# horses, yesterday? I was fine here until them, man. They broke my nerve. That's it, man. I've had it. I'm out of here." He slammed a large log onto the ground and started down the road.

I followed behind him, calling out to him. It's times like this that I feel like a fake. My prayers become short and desperate. I prayed, "Lord, I don't know what to do here! Help!"

Harvey stopped by an abandoned van near the barn. After I caught up with him, I sat down in the van's open cargo door and Harvey paced back and forth.

"Go on, man," he fumed. "You can send me back to Chicago right now. I'm pissed off at this whole place. Those horses yesterday broke me, man."

The previous afternoon Harvey had been afraid to ride a horse. When we take a guy up to this camp, one of my goals is getting him to try new things. Difficult things. And when he accomplishes those new and difficult things, we help him apply those lessons to his life in the city. If a guy can find the courage to overcome fear of horses, the climbing wall, the hiking or the skiing, maybe he can find the courage to overcome other fears and addictions. But Harvey didn't see it that way. He had gotten past his fear, but continued to rage. He couldn't deal with his feelings.

"I'm twenty-two now," he said as he paced. "My brother and uncle who raised me are dead. I gots no one. Ever since I was eleven I would get high with pot. I'll tell you the truth, man. Even on the streets, anytime I feel like hurting someone, I go get high. But you won't let me do that up here, so what am I suppose to do? That *&%# Shelton comes near me today, I'm going to kill him!"

Harvey's anger was typical of many of our guys. I had learned to cope with feelings by observing my parents and siblings as I grew up: how to express anger correctly, how to manage frustration, where and when to vent appropriately. When you live in a healthy household, you learn these things by example. But Harvey and many of our other guys never had those examples.

Compared to other men, guys like Harvey — guys who hustle — are more likely to have had parents or siblings who abused drugs or alcohol. Generally, they've also had significantly earlier sexual experiences and, often, an older first sexual partner who was male. Do these ingredients make for a happy life? Obviously not. It's not surprising that research confirms that these guys are usually more depressed, have fewer dreams for a career, and are more likely to struggle with alcohol or drug addictions themselves.[9]

Harvey moved back and forth like a wild animal trapped in a cage. I reached into my bag of "de-escalation tricks" and tried humor, misdirection, reasoning, and even threats. Nothing helped. He just continued to get more and more angry. Finally, in desperation I asked him, "Harvey, can I pray for you?"

He stopped. Without waiting for his reply, I got up, took his head between my hands, bowed my head, and prayed. I prayed that God would show himself to Harvey and show him how to deal with his anger. I prayed that the Holy Spirit would fill Harvey with courage and dispel his rage. I prayed for Harvey and how lost he felt in the world. I prayed that he would open himself to God's love. Tears welled in my eyes and my nose got stuffy. I felt Harvey's tenseness and I continued praying for him and for the easing of his pain. I ended by saying a benediction and tracing the Sign of the Cross on his forehead.

We each took a step back, and I asked him if we could return to work. He said, "Sure," and off we went. I didn't see any drastic change in him, but I thought the rage was gone.

We finished our morning's wood chopping without further incident, and Harvey seemed calm. At lunch, Shelton sat at another table. Near the end of our meal, I saw Harvey approach him. I tensed up and watched out of the corner of my eye. Harvey stuck out his hand and apologized. Shelton said he was sorry for mouthing off, and we headed back to our cabin.

In the cabin, Harvey handed Shelton a beautiful Eddie Bauer down winter coat he had found in our free clothing room just before the trip. It was a treasure.

"Shelton, I'm really sorry for what I did," he said quietly. "I want you to have this."

Shelton thanked him for the coat, and Harvey walked away.

* * * *

Back in the city, I reflected on that incident at camp. On a very real level, I'll never fully understand what these guys have gone through in life. I've never been drunk, never been high, and never had to sell my body on the streets to survive. And I'm more than fairly certain guys like Harvey and Shelton didn't experience too many kind strangers comforting them with free comic books and ice cream cones.

I came away from our trip to the north woods with a couple of lessons learned.

One: If I'm going to step into these guys' cages, prayer needs to come first. I can get prideful and think I have all the answers, but none of my "tools" or "skills" did Harvey any good. What I resorted to in desperation — prayer — was what I should have turned to first. I felt as if God had tapped me on the shoulder and said, "Excuse me, mind if I give it a try?"

Two: I was reminded that courage comes from proximity. Too often we can put physical things between us and the people to whom God wants us to minister. Perhaps it's a tract or pamphlet; our office hours; or our large, imposing desk. But the fear and rage that these men carry isn't going to be healed through these props. The healing happens through a person who's willing to step into a guy's cage, take some shocks, and remain present in the midst of his pain.

Many times it was with His touch that Jesus healed people of their blindness, lameness, leprosy, and more. Throughout Galilee and Judea, Christ's physical touch and proximity were the vehicles God used to bring outer and inner healing.

When I was scared and fearful as an "abandoned" young boy, I found courage in the comforting touch, kind words, and presence of strangers. Simple acts perhaps, but ones that can make a great difference in a young boy's life and in the life of a guy like Harvey, too, if only we're willing to step into his cage.

Digging Deeper

Listen and Reflect

Listen to "Lay It Down" at www.greenchoby.com/music-5.html. That initial act of "stepping into the cage" can also mean stepping away from what is familiar. It can often be a step into the unknown. Laying down our fears and insecurities is the first act in stepping into the cage.

Read and Reflect

In Matthew 9:18-33, we see how Jesus' proximity and touch resulted in healing and courage through raising a woman from the dead, restoring sight to two blind men, and expelling a demon. Consider what challenges the Lord faced in ministering this way. Think for a moment what concerns His friends had about what He was doing.

For Discussion

Viv Grigg, an evangelical missionary in Indonesia, wrote this in his book titled *Companion to the Poor*:

Disciple making is the transmission of life to life. It is caught, not taught. It is a fire that breeds fire. It is not a method, a program, nor even the teaching and preaching of the Word of God — though all of these are involved. Disciple making is God's love being poured out through one life into another, until the second life catches that love.

1. How are you active in transmitting faith to others?

2. What keeps you from "stepping into the cage" of the poor?

Pray

"Jesus, help me overcome the fear of proximity to those who make me feel uncomfortable — the homeless person I pass on the street, the African refugee who speaks only halting English at the supermarket, the Pakistani clerk wearing a turban at the cash register of the local gas station."

Chapter 4

The Ragman's Gift

Spiritual direction, an ancient discipline of the Christian Church, is the act of accompanying a person in their conversion and ongoing pursuit of holiness. It's a practice that I've found tremendously helpful in keeping me centered on Christ and spiritually renewed for the task at hand.

My spiritual director for several years was a wonderful Catholic woman named Martha Bartholomew. Martha and her husband, David, run Siloam, a Christian retreat center outside of Chicago. For many years, it was an oasis of peace and calm for me in the midst of the stress and clamor of urban life and ministry.

Martha once shared this story with me:

A man dies and appears before St. Peter at the pearly gates of heaven. St. Peter looks at the fellow and says, "Before I can let you in, I need you to roll up your sleeves." The man is puzzled, but does as he is asked. St. Peter examines the man's arms and asks, "Where are your scars?" Still confused, the man answers, "I don't have any scars." With tears in his eyes, St. Peter asks him, "Was nothing worth fighting for?"

I think I've gotten some of my best scars on Christmas Eve.

* * * *

His eyes stared past me into the distance. His face was rough and dark, weathered and sad. I knew his thin, torn blanket provided little comfort. Crumbs sprinkled his beard, which was flecked with gray, betraying his age. He was a ragman lying on a cement sidewalk in an "emerald city" — the name locals use for this underground street.

As I approached him, a trembling hand in a fingerless glove reached out to me while his glazed eyes continued to stare over my shoulder at something unseen. Two of the man's own fingers were missing and the fingernails on the remaining three were rotten and cracked. Deep lines etched their way down each of the three fingers. When I placed a brightly wrapped Christmas present into that ragged hand, the shiny box trembled slightly, too. Its clean, neat bow stood out in stark contrast to his filthy clothes and ragged appearance. The box held only a few pairs of socks, some toiletries, and a candy cane, but he cradled it as if it were a newborn child.

I returned to our car and drove on, but I couldn't get the vacant stare and weathered face of the Ragman out of my mind.

That Christmas Eve, Laura (one of our volunteers), Carolyn and I distributed more than fifty Christmas presents — one by one — to people on the streets.

Our first stop was Halsted Street where much of our ministry among young men occurs. The night was freezing and we were bundled up. Each of us carried a blue backpack loaded with gifts. Santa would have been proud.

After walking the block for a while without seeing any hustlers, we decided to stop by a few gay bars where we minister. As Laura and Carolyn went around the block one more time, I headed into "Cheeks." It's a small, dark place with a piano in a back corner. That night it was about half-filled, smoky, and — as always — dimly lit. I walked up to the bar and called to the bartender.

"Hi, I'm with Emmaus Minis . . . "

"I know who you are," he cut me off with disdain.

We hadn't had the easiest time gaining acceptance here. The previous summer the owner asked us to stay out. Since the fall, a few of us had been going back in. A bar like Cheeks is a wonderful place for us to be. It's a place that needs the relentless tenderness of Jesus. The men here are looking for a relationship that won't abandon them. Often they seek fulfillment in rented love with one of the guys we work with. That's why hustlers frequent this bar, preying on the men's desire to be loved; and the men prey on the hustlers' need to earn cash. All are wounded in the process.

The bartender stared at me.

"I have some Christmas presents here I would like to give you."

He stepped back, surprised. I pulled out three presents (a sweater, gloves, and a scarf, I think) and handed them across the counter.

"If you see someone tonight who needs a little Christmas cheer, give them one of these."

He accepted the gifts and smiled.

"Hey, that's a great idea," he said, thanking me.

I left Cheeks and walked next door to "Brewers." This bar is larger and has pool tables and dartboards. In the corners, televisions hanging from the ceiling play gay porn films. I was greeted warmly by several guys I know, and I handed a batch of presents to the bartender. After talking for a bit, I left.

Often the men in these bars get only insults and rejection from Christians. But through the years, they've witnessed our efforts at reaching young guys on the streets and have responded positively to our presence. As opportunities arise, we are able to tell them about Jesus and share our faith. These are great places to minister.

When Laura, Carolyn and I regrouped, we drove to Chicago's business area, "the Loop." For several decades a few blocks there have been known for male prostitution. Most of the guys' clients are business people coming to and from work, conventioneers in town for the weekend, and suburbanites in the city for a quick "trick."

On one corner is a bank of pay phones the guys stand at and pretend to use. The phones provide them with an excuse for being on the corner in case the cops drive by. Across the street is a large restaurant once owned by the Chicago Bulls' legendary Michael Jordan. (A huge Spalding basketball used to adorn the roof and a twenty-foot mural of Jordan decorated the front wall.) The restaurant exudes the success and wealth that is an unimaginable goal for the young men across the street on the phone.

That Christmas Eve, we saw seven or eight guys hustling at the phones.

One face was very familiar, though I hadn't seen him in a couple of years. Gerome was back on the street, just released from prison. With no family and no place to go, hustling downtown was the only way he could think of to get some money. We talked and I encouraged him to come by Emmaus for our Christmas dinner. I handed him a present and left.

After talking with the other guys and giving them presents, too, we drove to Lower Wacker Drive. This underground road rings the Loop. Delivery drivers and Chicago natives take it as a shortcut through downtown. It's nicknamed "the emerald city" because it was once lined with green fluorescent lights. A few years ago the drive was renovated. It's not as grimy now — and the emerald lights are gone — but homeless people still make its nooks and crannies into their temporary homes. For some, it's a last stop before dying from exposure, violence, alcohol, or disease.

On that December night, dark, gray icicles of frozen street runoff hung from the ceiling and the air was thick with diesel and gasoline fumes. On the same sidewalks that commuters scurried over by day, the homeless now clustered in groups of five or ten for protection from gangs and drunks. While this underground street is wide, accommodating the hundreds of trucks that pass through each day, its sidewalks are narrow. That night they were crowded with almost two hundred homeless people.

I've done this Christmas Eve outreach for several years, and each year it still amazes me that so many people are homeless in a country with so much wealth and so many resources. In 2007 the National Law Center on Homelessness and Poverty reported that as many as 3.5 million people, equal to the entire population of the State of Oregon, are likely to experience homelessness in a given year. Nearly 1.35 million of these homeless are children.

A section of Lower Wacker Drive that lies under a posh hotel is prime nighttime real estate in cold weather. Exhaust ducts from the hotel push up warm air through vents beside the slender sidewalk. The homeless fight for the right to sleep next to one.

We dropped a few presents next to huddled masses buried deep beneath blankets, cardboard, and newspaper.

This is where I encountered the Ragman, offered the present, and saw the three-fingered, weathered hand take the gift without our eyes ever meeting.

* * * *

In the gleaming city above the emerald city, families gathered around their ornamented trees, children dreamed of the jolly guy in the red suit, and church sanctuaries were filled with poinsettias. Why is it that in the Ragman's presence, in a brief encounter with a man who never met my eyes . . . . Why is it *there* that I felt the presence of Jesus?

I walk away from evenings like that Christmas Eve filled with pain. It's hard to see someone like the Ragman on the street, the men in bars medicating their loneliness, or the guys hustling on Hubbard Street. I don't know if our acts of kindness do any good.

I do know I leave these nights with a few scars.

The Ragman still touches my soul.

Digging Deeper

Listen and Reflect

Listen to "Sleep Tonight" at www.greenchoby.com/music-16.html. During the following fall after our winter encounter with the Ragman, Carolyn was walking our dog through a nearby park and encountered a homeless person sitting on a bench. She wrote this song after she got home.

Read and Reflect

The prophet Isaiah says, "If you remove the yoke from among you, the pointing of the finger, the speaking of evil, if you offer your food to the hungry and satisfy the needs of the afflicted, then your light shall rise in the darkness and your gloom be like the noonday" (Is 58:9-10).

This might be my favorite passage of Scripture. I love that it says nothing about the results of these works of mercy. It doesn't say that if you feed the hungry they will never be hungry again. It doesn't say that if you satisfy the needs of the oppressed there will no longer be injustice. It simply says that if *you* do these works of mercy, *your* light will break forth; *your* darkness will be like noonday. When we do God's justice, we are the ones who are changed.

For Discussion

In 1938, George MacLeod founded the
Iona Community. Headquartered in Glasgow,
Scotland, it is an ecumenical Christian community
committed to issues of peace and justice.
Thoughts like this motivated him:

> I simply argue that the cross be raised again at the
> center of the marketplace, as well as on the steeple of
> the Church. I am recovering the claim that Jesus was not
> crucified in a cathedral between two candles, but on a
> cross between two thieves. On the town garbage heap.
> At a crossroad so cosmopolitan that they had to write
> His title in Hebrew and in Latin and in Greek. At the kind
> of place where cynics talk smut, and thieves curse and
> soldiers gamble. Because that is where He died and that
> is what He died about. And that is where Church people
> ought to be and what Church people should be about.

1. How does this quote relate to the Ragman story above?

2. What is worth fighting for to you?

3. Where are your scars?

Pray

"God of mercy and compassion, help us to one day
bring every homeless Ragman out of the darkness
and cold of the streets and into the warmth and
light of our homes."

Chapter 5

The Way Out of the Cage

Today when we think of a prophet, too often we envision a fortuneteller, a palm reader, or an old woman in a headscarf waving her gnarled hand over a crystal ball as she attempts to see the future. In the time of the prophet Micah, that wasn't the image. Only rarely does any prophet in Scripture speak to future events. The prophet's role was not to reveal the future, but to point people to the present — to spotlight where God's people fell short of His road map for living. But if that's all the prophets had done, they'd only qualify as village gossips who constantly nagged people about their shortcomings. Besides publicly declaring the people's sins, God's prophets highlighted the way forward, by asking pointed questions that demand heartfelt answers.

The first section of this book has reflected on Micah's initial question:

"What does the Lord require of you?" But that's not the end of this prophet's message. He goes on to shine a light on three ways to move forward: living justly, showing mercy, and walking humbly with God. We'll explore each in turn in the next three sections.

The guys we work with at Emmaus aren't very lovable. They don't naturally engender a compassionate response. They're not young kids ravaged by war, drought, or hurricanes. They don't generate much sympathy. Our world sees them as worthless and of no value at first glance.

And there's the problem. In our busy, modern world, we rarely take time to look beyond that first glance. If a person's story doesn't fit into the fifteen-second sound bite or three-second video image and immediately tug at our hearts, we dismiss it. And therein lies the path to "learned blindness." For me, avoiding this blindness has meant stepping into the cages of these guys, walking with them, and ultimately showing them the way out.

I believe God requires each of us to step into the cage. Perhaps it's not the cage of prostituting men. Perhaps your cage, your calling, is different. Regardless of what the cage looks like, we all need to heed the prophet's call.

No matter the particular cage, this is never a solitary process. I learned early on that I could do nothing for these men without the help of the Body of Christ. A host of tenderhearted people willing to step out of their own conditioning has walked alongside me to care for the poor. Some helped for a few months; some for a few years. Local churches and parishes around the country have supported our work, prayed for our men, and invited me to speak to their people. When I talk about our work, I often tell the story of Anthony.

* * * *

I knew Anthony for a couple of years. He loved coming to Emmaus but didn't like hearing our challenge to him to change his ways and turn his life around. He was respectful when we prayed before our meals and occasionally participated in a Bible study, but he made it clear that he didn't believe in God. Still, he kept dropping by, and we kept loving him and reaching out to him.

During that time the hazards of street life were rapidly catching up to him. By the age of forty his intravenous drug use, promiscuous sex, poor hygiene and eating habits, nightly prostitution, frequent homelessness, and incarceration had taken their toll. Anthony was living out the final hours of his life, his body ravaged by hepatitis and AIDS.

Many of the guys we work with at Emmaus are HIV positive. For many people, HIV is manageable if . . . . they have access to good healthcare, are committed to eating right, can make frequent doctor visits, and are able to navigate through a social service system that will pay thousands of dollars monthly for the medication they need to stay alive. But for a guy on the streets, without those abilities and resources, becoming HIV positive is often a death sentence.

Infection rates continue to rise among Americans although the country spent more than $100 billion dollars in the past decade on HIV/AIDS prevention and treatment.[10] One recent study showed that "the prevalence of HIV infection within some U.S. populations now rivals that in some sub-Saharan African countries. For example, more than 1 in 30 adults in Washington, D.C., are HIV-infected — a prevalence higher than that reported in Ethiopia, Nigeria or Rwanda."[11]

Anthony was more than a statistic to us.

Amy, one of our staff members at the time, was ministering to Anthony both in and out of the hospital. She was also working with our ministry director, Sill Davis, to help him get his medical care and his other affairs in order. She even threw a special birthday party for him.

Amy was also taking Anthony to church on Sundays and to a healing service on Wednesday nights at Church of the Redeemer, an Anglican parish in Skokie, Illinois. Members of her congregation made Anthony feel welcome and gathered around him in prayer. But despite her best efforts, she felt that his heart was hardening to the Gospel as the fear of death set in.

Eventually, an infection took hold that ultimately ended Anthony's life. An ambulance rushed him to the hospital on a Friday morning. The doctors predicted he wouldn't make it through the weekend. We called family members, consisting of an aunt and a handful of cousins, to his bedside. Anthony's mother had passed away when he was a young teen and he didn't know his father. His big brother, who had guided him through much of his life, was now in jail. Anthony's lover, Michael; a drag queen he was friends with on the street; and a couple other street guys from Emmaus stood vigil in the ICU of Weiss Hospital in Chicago's Uptown.

Late Friday evening, Father Martin Mahoney from Church of the Redeemer arrived at the hospital. He asked Anthony, now drifting in and out of consciousness, whether he believed Jesus had died to save him. Anthony said he did, and that he also wanted to be baptized. In the ICU, with tubes running in and out of Anthony's body and electronic monitors humming and chirping, we held an intimate baptismal ceremony around his hospital bed. Later that evening, he slipped into a coma, then passed away the following day.

* * * *

Evangelical missionary C.T. Studd once said, "Some people want to live within the sound of chapel bells, but I want to run a mission a yard from the gates of hell." We stand with these men — and an increasing number of teenage boys — who, physically and spiritually, are teetering between life and death. (Because of violent tricks, the random dangers of the streets, serial killers — we do outreach in bars once frequented by John Wayne Gacy and Jeffrey Dahmer — drug overdoses, prison violence, or disease, most male hustlers don't survive past the age of forty.)

Rescuing an individual from the streets — and almost certain death — looks different in each man's life. For some it means helping them turn their lives around, finish school, obtain housing or find solid employment, and — hopefully — grounding them in a relationship with Christ and a church family outside of Emmaus. For others, it could mean earning a GED, obtaining a legal ID card, becoming responsible fathers, or breaking the cycle of prostitution and drug use. And for a precious few, like Anthony, it's the privilege of leading them to faith in Christ in the final moments of their lives.

One Lent I shared this story at a suburban Catholic parish and a woman at the front table stopped me with a look on her face like she was chewing nails. I asked her what was wrong.

"You shouldn't have done that!" she said through slightly clenched teeth.

"What shouldn't I have done?" I asked.

"You were proselytizing him on his deathbed! You were taking advantage of his situation. You shouldn't have asked him if he wanted to be baptized!"

For a moment I considered reminding her that it was Father Martin's invitation and not mine, but that would have been a cop-out. I've encountered attitudes like hers before. Some people believe that the poor should *never* be evangelized; that this is unfair proselytizing. Many church members are most comfortable living the faith by example and trusting in the power of that witness.

In his 1975 apostolic exhortation *Evangelii Nuntiandi* (On Evangelization in the Modern World), Pope Paul VI wrote:

> Above all the Gospel must be proclaimed by witness. Take a Christian or a handful of Christians who, in the midst of their own community, show their capacity for understanding and acceptance, their sharing of life and destiny with other people, their solidarity with the efforts of all for whatever is noble and good. Let us suppose that, in addition, they radiate in an altogether simple and unaffected way their faith in values that go beyond current values, and their hope in something that is not seen and that one would not dare to imagine. Through this wordless witness, these Christians stir up irresistible questions in the hearts of those who see how they live: Why are they like this? Why do they live in this way? What or who is it that inspires them? Why are they in our midst? Such a witness is already a silent proclamation of the Good News and a very powerful and effective one.[12]

The vast majority of us who claim Christ as our Savior are satisfied with stopping there. But the pope continued:

> Nevertheless this always remains insufficient, because even the finest witness will prove ineffective in the long run if it is not explained, justified — what Peter called always having "your answer ready for people who ask you the reason for the hope that you all have" — and made explicit by a clear and unequivocal proclamation of the Lord Jesus. The Good News proclaimed by the witness of life sooner or later has to be proclaimed by the word of life. There is no true evangelization if the name, the teaching, the life, the promises, the kingdom and the mystery of Jesus of Nazareth, the Son of God are not proclaimed.[13]

The most violent act we can commit against someone who is poor is to *not* tell him or her about Jesus.

When Anthony slipped from this life into heaven, we could have stopped there and rejoiced over the return of this prodigal son to the Father. But we've learned from walking with guys like Anthony in the final moments of their lives that we have an amazing opportunity afterward to minister to their families. We came alongside Anthony's family members, few of whom had a church background or had the financial resources to cover even a simple burial. The week after he died, our staff organized a memorial service and reception in his honor. We wrote the obituary, planned the program, ministered to the family, and took advantage of the opportunity to talk about Christ, death, and reconciliation with loved ones. A bunch of our men, Anthony's friends, prepared the food for the reception that followed the service.

The memorial service was held a block from our ministry, at Uptown Baptist Church. This congregation is known for its racial and ethnic diversity, evangelistic presence in the community, and social services. Uptown Baptist hosts a women's shelter in the basement and a soup kitchen that feeds four hundred to five hundred people on Monday nights. Considering the funeral a part of its ministry, the church graciously opened its facilities to us.

The service itself was a moving tribute. Family members and friends (and a couple of homeless people who randomly wandered in off the streets) shared colorful stories about Anthony. Our office manager, Isaiah Evans, sang a beautiful rendition of "My Soul is Anchored in the Lord." Pastor Roger Mahoney shared a powerful eulogy and Gospel presentation. Members from Church of the Redeemer who once ministered to Anthony attended the service and also brought food for the reception.

In the aftermath of the funeral, we were struck by how the death of this one man exalted Christ and demonstrated the Gospel in the lives of so many individuals. We also felt honored to extend abundant kindness to Anthony's family, friends, and partner.

In the world's economy, many would view reaching out to these broken men as a "lost cause" or at least unworthy of time or financial backing. God's economy is different. In His eyes, the orphan in Romania, the Angolan refugee, the wealthy suburban businessman, the farmer's wife in Kentucky, and the man prostituting on the streets of Chicago are equally loved and valued. He longs for each one of these prodigal sons and daughters — each one of us — to come to a saving knowledge of Christ.

I doubt Anthony's life turned out the way he wanted it. Like all of our men, he lived on the margins of society. Thankfully, in spite of our own poor choices and the brokenness of life, we have a heavenly Father who sees our hearts and our potential.

I'm grateful to work with people like Amy and Sill, who reflect God's love to these men not only in words but also in actions. I'm also thankful for our partnerships with churches such as Uptown Baptist and St. Thomas of Canterbury in our neighborhood, our friends at Church of the Redeemer, and other congregations who faithfully support Emmaus. While I strive to incarnate Christ, I'm insufficient as an individual. It takes a community of believers at Emmaus and multiple churches to reflect the fullness of God's kingdom to men like Anthony.

It was painful stepping into Anthony's cage. Journeying with him meant taking some shocks and getting some scars. Thankfully, even at the moment of his death, we were able to show him the way out of his cage. Perhaps our greatest prophetic witness at Emmaus is to point out to the church and to society that men like Anthony have worth and value.

Digging Deeper

Listen and Reflect

The song "Narrow," written by Mike Choby, reflects the hearts yearning to walk with God when the road gets narrow. Listen to it by visiting www.greenchoby.com/music-13.html.

Read and Reflect

The Streets I Feared To See

I said: "Let me walk in the field," God said: "Nay, walk in the town."
I said: "There are no flowers there," He said: "No flowers but a crown."
I said: "But the sky is black and there is nothing but noise and din,"
But He wept as He sent me back, "There is more," He said "there is sin."
I said: "But the air is thick and fogs are veiling the sun."
He answered: "Yet souls are sick, and souls in the dark undone."
I said: "I shall miss the light, and friends will miss me, they say,"
He answered me: "Choose tonight, if I am to miss you, or they."
I pleaded for time to be given; He said: "Is it hard to decide?
It will not seem hard in Heaven, to have followed the steps of your guide."
I cast one look at the fields, and then set my face to the town.
He said: "My child, do you yield? Will you leave the flowers for the crown?"
Then into His hand went mine, and into my heart came He;
and I walk in a light Divine, the streets I had feared to see."
— George MacDonald (1824-1905)

Consider how this poem challenges you to step beyond your own conditioning.

For Discussion

"But God has so arranged the body, giving the greater honor to the inferior member, that there may be no dissension within the body, but the members may have the same care for one another. If one member suffers, all suffer together with it; if one member is honored, all rejoice together with it" (1 Cor 12:24-26).

1. Anthony was ministered to by an ecumenical group of believers. Why is this type of cross-denominational evangelization difficult in our day?

2. Where do you see such evangelization happening?

3. What sorts of cages is God asking you to step into today?

Pray

"Beloved Father, help me place my hand in Yours and step into the unknown with the knowledge that You are at my side and giving purpose to my steps."

Section II

How Can I Live Justly?

He has showed you, O man, what is good.
And what does the LORD require of you?
To act justly
and to love mercy
and to walk humbly with your God.

— Micah 6:8, NIV

For me, answering the question from Micah 6:8 about how to live justly has meant adopting an incarnational approach to ministry and life. Justice in Holy Scripture implies using all that we have and all that we are: the relationships, connections, resources, and abilities God has given us, to live in right relationship with Him, those around us, and the world. I think this Chinese proverb captures an incarnational model of ministry:

Go to the People,
Live among them.
Learn from them.
Serve them.
Plan with them.
Start with what they know.
Build with what they have.

Chapter 6

"I'm a Pimp, I'm Not a Cowboy!"

I realize now that choosing where I live is one of the most important "justice decisions" that I will ever make.

When I was growing up, my home was in crime-free, suburban Silver Lake, Ohio, with my parents. When I went to college in small-town Wheaton, Illinois, I lived in the dorms and enjoyed weekend strolls down Main Street to Dairy Queen or the small movie theater in town. During my college summers, I rented apartments near my church in Wheaton because it was convenient for my job as a youth minister.

In 1989, I returned from my New York City sojourn in street outreach to finish my undergrad degree and start graduate school. I moved into a large two-bedroom apartment with some other grad students in the

Chicago suburbs, just north of Wheaton. The large apartment building on Gundersen Avenue was located near my part-time night job at the hospital, multiple restaurants ideal for "cooking-challenged" young adult such as myself, and Wheaton Graduate School. Convenience, ease, and proximity were the deciding factors of where I lived.

In the fall of 1990, I eased my way into urban living. I first moved into an apartment that my mentor, Rev. Mark Van Houten, was vacating. I had walked Chicago streets with Mark for about a year and was starting Emmaus Ministries when he and his wife decided to relocate out of state. Their large, three-bedroom apartment was on Chicago's northwest side only two minutes from the Kennedy Expressway.

It was an ideal transitional location for me. Being close to the expressway made my suburban commute to the hospital and graduate school a simple thirty minutes, plus living in the city gave me easier access to my developing ministry on Chicago's north side. The biggest problem I faced in my tree-lined, residential neighborhood was finding street parking when I came home at three o'clock in the morning after a night of outreach.

A year in that apartment was a good segue. In the fall of 1991, my time and commitment to Emmaus were increasing and I was earning a part-time salary after two years of volunteering. With my graduate schoolwork almost complete, I decided to move closer to the ministry. It was the first time I chose a place to live that was not based on convenience for my job or proximity to school.

The Uptown neighborhood on Chicago's north side, about a mile north of Wrigley Field, seemed a perfect community for expanding Emmaus. Uptown was close to the main area where I was reaching men in prostitution. It was a diverse community where white and minority, gay and straight, young and old, could come and go without neighbors batting an eye. And it was poor and affordable.

That fall two friends and I rented a large, three-bedroom apartment there. The building owners lived on the first floor and had recently renovated the whole three-story, three-unit building. Our second-floor apartment had new hardwood floors and quality Anderson windows. Our building was nothing like the crack house, public-housing high-rises, and run-down rentals that surrounded it. After only a few months, we started inviting guys to drop by for help in their getting off the streets or just for a good meal or shower. Soon it became the center for our growing ministry.

My new home brought me much closer to guys I was working with. No longer did I only see them hustling at night in "boys town." Now, for example, I ran into them at the local supermarket. The nearby church I joined, St. Thomas of Canterbury, had a soup kitchen twice a week where I volunteered. Almost every night, one of the guys I knew on the streets reached out for the bowl of soup I offered. Sometimes, when I was getting off the subway at the Wilson Avenue Red Line stop, I passed one of the guys heading downtown and we chatted.

Ministry to these men was no longer something I did once, twice, or three times a week; now it was a part of daily life. This intentionality also immersed me in the "low-intensity conflict" of urban life.

* * * *

It was 1:15 a.m. A few minutes before I was in my kitchen washing dishes and sweating in Chicago's stifling humidity and sweltering summer heat. The back door was propped open in the hopes of catching at least a faint summer breeze.

I wouldn't have heard the gun shots if it had been closed.

"Fireworks?" I wondered. No. The distinctive "pop, pop, pop" of small arms fire is unmistakable. Soon after the shots, the slight wind carried the sounds of screaming and police sirens.

I was haunted by what I had read earlier that afternoon in a book by Jim Wallace, editor of *Sojourners* magazine. Wallace made this observation:

> Several weeks after the Los Angeles events [race riots], a friend wrote to me, saying, "Watching the painful images of Los Angeles in flames caused me to think of your community, always living in the middle of a low-intensity riot." The image has stuck with me. We have seen wars of low-intensity conflict in places such as El Salvador, South Africa, and the Philippines. But what is happening all the time in South Central L.A., inner-city Washington, D.C., and in countless other urban cauldrons of human suffering across America can, in truth, be termed a low-intensity riot.[14]

Young people ages eighteen to twenty-four experience the highest homicide rates in our country. While drug arrests for juveniles have remained steady for the last forty years, arrests for adults have skyrocketed. This has led to incarceration rates rising more than 400 percent since the 1980s. These statistics, and many like them, paint a grim picture. [15]

Such is life in the city — and the low intensity conflict of the streets.

Just two weeks before this I had been in the peaceful north woods of Wisconsin. What a contrast! My roommate Brian Wells, an Emmaus volunteer, and I had driven four guys from the streets up to HoneyRock Camp.

Charlie was one of them.

* * * *

I first met Charlie on Broadway in Uptown. A large, muscular guy with a no-nonsense look on his face, Charlie was imposing. He was pimping a young girl named Jamie. She was a very naïve eighteen-year-old from the suburbs. After seeing Jamie and Charlie together a couple of times, I was eventually able to catch a few moments alone with her. Something I said must have sunk in because a week later Charlie stormed up to me. "Brother John! I'm really mad! After talking with you, Jamie left me and went back to her parents. Now what am I gonna do?"

A year passed and during that time Charlie had been getting high or drunk almost every night and doing whatever he could to earn a buck — pimping, panhandling, even prostituting himself.

I ran into him on the street one night and told him I was taking a bunch of guys up to a camp in Wisconsin as a time to get away from the streets and to think about where their lives were heading. Charlie agreed to go.

At the camp, I made sure that he and the other guys tried new experiences.

Like horseback riding.

At the stables, I showed the guys the horses they would be riding. Our small group, as well as a larger equestrian class from Wheaton College, milled around the "tack shack" getting helmets, saddles, and bridles. Our inner-city group of rough-looking guys contrasted with the young, perfect-teethed, and designer-clothed kids from Wheaton.

I watched as Charlie reluctantly approached his horse. He managed to get through the grooming and saddling but still seemed nervous. This was a new experience for him. After the preliminaries, our horses were lined up along the fence with the college students' horses on the other side. I helped Charlie into the stirrup and he mounted FOP (short for "Fat Old Pony"). Charlie's eyes were wide with fear, but he seemed all right, so I turned to help another guy.

A few seconds later FOP pulled its left front hoof back a step and dove its snout into the snow looking for something to munch. Charlie felt this animal move underneath him and started to panic. As Charlie's fears escalated, he begged for help off the beast. I used every persuasive argument I could think of to get him to stay on. Finally, at the end of his wits and with fists raised, Charlie turned to me and in a terrified, desperate voice screamed, "DAMN IT, JOHN. I'M A PIMP, I'M NOT A COWBOY!"

At that instant, the equestrian class from Wheaton College emerged from the tack shack. I looked up and saw all of them standing still, staring dumbstruck at Charlie and me, all of them resembling deer caught in the headlights of a car. And with that, I helped him down as FOP continued its snack.

Shortly after we returned from camp, Charlie entered a Christian rehab program called Chicago Victory Center. He stayed there for almost a year as he got his life together. We kept in touch through the ensuing months of his recovery.

About three years after Charlie had stormed up to me on the street, I watched as he read one of the Scripture passages at my wedding. This former pimp and prostitute had turned his life around.

* * * *

The "low intensity conflict" of our inner cities tries to kill men like Charlie. Some are able to break free, but others get mired in violence, drugs, prostitution, and gangs.

To reach guys like these, I chose an apartment location that brought me into closer proximity with their lives. "Go to the people, live among them" is a model we see in the Incarnation. Christ came into our world of chaos and conflict and dealt among us. Redemption, healing, and resurrection all came from His intentional Incarnation. As a follower of Jesus, I need to exercise the same intentionality in choosing where I will live. Despite the pressures of the world to make this choice based upon my own ease and convenience, I need to realize it's a "justice decision" and one I must make after much prayer and discernment.

Digging Deeper

Listen and Reflect

Carolyn wrote the song "Highlight" after one of our guys told her he had been clean and sober from drugs for almost three months. With an addiction measured by the decade, three months was indeed something worth celebrating. Listen to the song at www.greenchoby.com/music-6.html.

Read and Reflect

"Make my joy complete: be of the same mind, having the same love, being in full accord and of one mind. Do nothing from selfish ambition or conceit, but in humility regard others as better than yourselves. Let each of you look not to your own interests, but to the interests of others. Let the same mind be in you that was in Christ Jesus" (Phil 2:2-5).

For Discussion

My Lord God, I have no idea where I am going. I
do not see the road ahead of me. I cannot know
for certain where it will end. Nor do I really know
myself, and the fact that I think that I am following
your will does not mean that I am actually doing
so. But I believe that the desire to please you does in fact
please you. And I hope I have that desire in all that I am
doing. I hope that I will never do anything apart from
that desire. And I know that if I do this you will lead me
by the right road, though I may know nothing about it.
Therefore will I trust you always though I may seem to
be lost and in the shadow of death. I will not fear, for you
are ever with me, and you will never leave me to face my
perils alone.

— Thomas Merton, *Thoughts in Solitude*

1. How can you choose to live an incarnational way of life?

2. How can you develop a deep trust in God and a willingness to
   let go and step into the unknown?

3. What in your day-to-day life makes this hard?

4. When the "still small voice" of the Spirit is drowned out by the
   noise and chaos of modern life, how and where do you find your
   center?

Pray

"Jesus, I trust in You."

Chapter 7

Walking Justly Together

Jesus sent His disciples out in pairs to minister. For good reason. From the very beginning of our work, I realized that reaching men prostituting on the streets was not something I could do alone. Also, in my own spiritual life, as I was asking, "How can I live justly?" it dawned on me that attempting an incarnational life of ministry would be impossible to do by myself. I needed my brothers and sisters. I needed the Church in all its division and brokenness. I needed close companions on this journey. Along these lines, the gifted spiritual writer, Father Henri Nouwen wrote:

> I have found over and over again how hard it is to
> be truly faithful to Jesus when I am alone. I need my
> brothers and sisters to pray with me, to speak with
> me about the spiritual task at hand, and to challenge

me to stay pure in mind, heart and body. But far more importantly, it is Jesus who heals, not I; Jesus who is Lord, not I. This is very clearly made visible when we proclaim the redeeming power of God together. Indeed, whenever we minister together, it is easier for people to recognize that we do not come in our own name, but in the name of the Lord Jesus who sent us."[16]

Personally, Father Nouwen's words always remind me how my wife, Carolyn, has blessed me throughout the mission of Emmaus. She has prayed with me, spoken to me about the spiritual task at hand, and constantly challenged me to stay pure. I haven't always listened, and we've had our challenges, but throughout it all, I have been tremendously thankful that the Lord has allowed us to journey together.

* * * *

Carolyn "stalked" me before we even started dating. I was a graduate student and she was an undergrad who . . . just happened to be sitting in the graduate school lounge every Tuesday and Thursday morning when my second-period class was finished. I'd walk by and she would throw me a very casual and innocent, "Oh, hi, John." When I took an evening class called "Writing for Ministry," she was one of the few undergrads to sign up for the graduate level course.

And then during a school-organized bicycling trip along the Mississippi River, she conveniently crashed her bike, causing me to rescue her. It was a beautiful, windless day, on a newly paved stretch of road; suspicious circumstances for wrecking her bike! Clearly, she was trying to get my attention.

Actually, I think it was the crash that caused me to consider asking her out. I was cycling just ahead of her and heard the sound. It looked pretty bad. She had instinctively stretched her arms out to break her fall on the pavement. This gouged up her hands. Her left elbow and chin also broke her fall, leading to other cuts and scrapes. By the time I had turned around, biked to where she had crashed, dug out a first-aid kit from my handlebar bag, and reached her, she was kneeling on the ground with her hands held up and blood dripping from several wounds.

When I knelt down, all she said was, "I'm sorry." Wow, I thought. No tears, no crying. She simply apologized for the inconvenience her crash was having on the trip.

Then a ray of sunlight reflected from her eye and I beheld a wounded angel. Heavenly voices reached a crescendo in song, and a warmth spread throughout my whole being. This is the woman I will marry!

No, it didn't really happen like that. Actually, I was a little upset that this stupid undergrad had spoiled a perfectly good day of biking. I *was* impressed that she wasn't crying. She seemed tough.

A couple of months after the accident, Carolyn asked to come down and volunteer with this growing ministry I was doing on the streets of Chicago. She fit right in and was great with the guys on the street.

We started dating sometime after that and married in February 1993, but these next two stories are about when we were first engaged.

* * * *

On a snowy afternoon in early winter somewhere along Indiana's State Route 85, Carolyn, a young man from the streets named Jimmy, and I were returning to Chicago after attending the wedding of a former outreach volunteer. We decided to stop for a dinner break at a truck stop, and as we waited for our burgers, Jimmy began talking about the wedding, obviously still thrilled that he had been invited.

The previous day he'd dropped by our ministry in the Uptown neighborhood and I let him pick out a suit from our clothing room. He looked "fresh," as they say on the streets, in his first suit.

I had been spending a lot of time with Jimmy, who had been hustling on the streets since the previous summer. He had told me of growing up in one foster home after another, his experiences on the streets, and his desire to change things around.

A United States Department of Justice article by Michael Scott and Kelly Dedel describe men who resort to prostitution this way:

> Street prostitutes have lower status than indoor prostitutes. They are often in some state of personal decline (e.g., running away from abusive situations, becoming drug-dependent, deteriorating psychologically and/or getting less physically attractive). Most have social, economic, and health problems. Most first turn to prostitution at a young age, often before they are 18. . . . Many prostitutes try to leave the streets,

although they often return and then leave again. Most return to prostitution because their limited education and lack of skills make finding employment very difficult. Without a means to support themselves and their children, they may think staying on the streets is less risky than leaving prostitution."[17]

That had been the case with Jimmy. He had tried to leave the streets and prostitution but kept falling back.

On the morning of the wedding, before the three of us had headed out from Chicago, I had asked him to say a prayer for us. The young man had had us bow our heads, and then he asked God to watch out for us on our trip to Indianapolis. Now, in the diner, the waitress brought us our food and we gave thanks. After Jimmy told us a few of his usual jokes, I got down to business. "Jimmy, how serious are you about your faith? I've heard you pray — at meals and before this trip — and was just wondering what God meant to you."

"I'm a bit confused" was his solemn response.

He began to tell us about the variety of Christians that he had met. People at the mission where he sometimes found shelter. People who witnessed on the street corners. His mom's neighbors. All those different varieties of Christian folk puzzled him.

"I don't really understand it all," he said. "I believe in Jesus and know that He was God's Son, but I don't understand these denominations."

I laughed a bit inside. You see, Carolyn is Baptist and I'm Catholic. We certainly seemed an appropriate couple for him to be asking about this.

"Jimmy," I said, "you're in the Gangster Disciples gang, right?"

"Yeah, that's straight." (Meaning "yes.")

"How do you know what neighborhoods you can or can't walk in, what colors you can or can't wear, or who the leader of each gang is?"

"Well, you just sorta grow up knowing them."

"What if," I continued, "you could put all the dos and don'ts and colors and important people and all the stuff about gangs in a book? If you knew this book, you could walk wherever you wanted in the city and not get confused, right?"

"Yeah, that's straight," he again agreed.

"Well, you know what, Jimmy? The Bible is God's gang book for Christians. It tells us what we need to know to walk through this world. It tells us about important people who started our faith and gave their lives for it. It keeps us from getting confused when things are confusing around us."

I asked Jimmy if he had read God's gang book very much. He said he hadn't, but would like to. I asked him if he'd get together with me to read it sometime. He said he'd try.

Good enough.

We returned to Chicago and dropped Jimmy off at his aunt's house where he lived.

A few days later, Carolyn and I visited our friend Charlie in a halfway house on the West Side of Chicago where he had been living for a year (see Chapter Six). As Carolyn and I pulled up to the rehab — a large, redbrick apartment building — we saw Charlie through the front-door window. As we entered, he gave us a big hug and I introduced my fiancée.

"You're marrying *him*!" he gasped. "I'll be praying for you, sister!" We all laughed.

We handed Charlie a couple of presents. He tore into the first one but stopped before opening the second. "You know, John," he said, "this is the first Christmas in thirteen years that I haven't been drunk or high. I miss it a bit, you know? But I know that this is where God wants me to be."

We stayed for a while, encouraging Charlie in his recovery. He had journeyed a long — hard — way, but the Lord had something good planned for this man, as He does all of us.

Before we left, we ask Charlie if he'd be willing to read one of the Scripture passages at our upcoming wedding. He said he would be privileged to do so. In my mind, it was far more our privilege to have this prodigal son be part of our life.

＊ ＊ ＊ ＊

We Christians sure are a funny bunch. We're confusing to a lot of people with our various denominations and ways of expressing ourselves. What's more confounding and distressing is the way we never seem to talk to one another. Yet ministries like Emmaus, which strive for a missional ecumenism, show it's possible for us to work together even though, admittedly, it's not always easy. The differences between the churches are vast and hotly contested. And too often, in our anger and confusion, we turn our backs on one another. However, through working together to reach young adult men on the street, we can build a bit of unity between separated brethren.

I have found it's hard for me "to be truly faithful to Jesus when I am alone." Not all of us find the seeds of that faithfulness to Christ in the Sacrament of Matrimony. But whatever our state in life, whether as a single person, vowed religious, priest, or married person, we all need community. Jesus never comes to us by himself. He brings His disciples, His saints, His mother, His whole Church. Neither does He expect us to face the challenging spiritual tasks at hand by ourselves. We need one another, desperately.

The divided Body of Christ is being called to work together. In his book titled *Your Church is Too Small*, Dr. John Armstrong calls this "missional ecumenism" and says it's been a growing phenomenon over the last fifty years. For example, since *Roe v. Wade* in 1973, evangelical Protestants, mainline Protestants, Roman Catholics, and Orthodox believers have been backing into each other on the sidewalks outside abortion clinics. This street-level ecumenism has fostered and blossomed into a variety of efforts that have carried us closer to the Lord's prayer that "they may be one" (Jn 17:11). From the start, Emmaus has been a wonderful expression of this missional ecumenism.

Digging Deeper

Listen and Reflect

Carolyn's song "Salt" speaks of the "brave lives from ancient times." We not only need one another today but also the Church throughout history to speak into our lives. Listen to "Salt" at www.greenchoby.com/music-41.html.

Read and Reflect

The following passage is from Haggai 1:7-11. Read it with the Church in mind:

> Thus says the Lord of hosts: Consider how you have fared. Go up to the hills and bring wood and build the house, so that I may take pleasure in it and be honored, says the Lord. You have looked for much, and, lo, it came to little; and when you brought it home, I blew it away. Why? says the Lord of hosts. Because my house lies in ruins, while all of you hurry off to your own houses. Therefore the heavens above you have withheld the dew, and the earth has withheld its produce. And I have called for a drought on the land and the hills, on the grain, the new wine, the oil, on what the soil produces, on human beings and animals, and on all their labors.

For Discussion

1. How do you see "living justly" and "missional ecumenism" relating?

2. In your community, do you see signs of the Body of Christ ministering together, beyond the normal divisions?

3. What about Jimmy's story stood out to you? Why?

Pray

"Father, help our divided Body better reflect Your heart of unity. Help us to find good companions on our journeys so that we may not walk alone."

Chapter 8

Buying a Crack House

Being married to a singer/songwriter has connected me with many independent musicians. I've discovered great bits of theology, philosophy, and insight in the hearts and souls of these artists. It's good food for the journey.

In his wonderful song "Waking Up," Minnesota-based singer/songwriter Peter Mayer tells the story of "Joe Somebody" waking up from the American Dream. The lyrics read:

> Last night I was dreaming I was in my GMC
> I was feeling kind of empty because it was just a '93
> So I filled it full of fossils from the bosom of the earth
> Which I burned up quite a lot of on my long commute to work

Where I worked at what I hated just to keep up with the bills
Which I paid to meet the rising cost of feeling unfulfilled
Which I felt at every moment with occasional respite
Like the times that I'd go shopping or watch TV shows at night

CHORUS: But I'm waking up, but I'm waking up
I'm waking up from the American Dream

Last night I was dreaming of the one eternal hope
That my life would be improved if the economy would grow
Which already was a monster on a mission to consume
And was eating almost everything and running out of room
And it whispered to me "mister, here's some products that you need
And the standard of your living is too low" and I agreed!
So I got myself a credit card with not a penny down
And a long ride on the not-so-merry-money-go-round,
CHORUS

Yeah, the world was like an Amoco and I said "Fill er up!"
With a house, a car, a VCR, a lawn and all that stuff
But I got a nagging notion that enough did not exist
And at the end of every day I'd wonder "is this all there is?"
And someone said "Hey, you've already got ten times more than the rest
And six-billion other people want the little that's still left!"
But I snapped "It's a free country and by rights it's mine to keep
And by the way, who do I pay to take away this garbage heap?"
CHORUS

It seemed that the beginning of the dream was so benign, I mean
All I ever wanted was a smidgen of the pie
And some comfort and security and good things for my kids
And, OK, to please the neighbors and my ego while I did
Anyway, it's great to be awake and feeling satisfied
With seeking out the simple and the deeper things in life
And with giving to the world instead of hoarding it for me
Boy, I guess I'm not too excited about falling back to sleep

And as crazy as it was, hey, was it a dream or not?
Well, just promise not to save me if I ever start to nod

Put no-doze in my coffee, throw me outside in the cold
Just don't ever say "OK now, back to bed you go!"
©Peter Mayer, www.blueboat.net18 (used with
permission)

I feel like I've been waking up slowly as I wrestle with Micah's question
of "How do I live justly?" Waking up to how materialism and consumerism
have affected my decision-making. Waking up to how the choices I make
impact people locally, nationally, and globally. Waking up to the need to
use in a just manner the resources God has given me.

During two decades of growing the ministry of Emmaus, I've run into
several people who have helped jolt me awake with hot, savory cups of
conviction on what it means to live justly.

I first met "The Bruised Camels" through Em Griffin, a communications
professor at Wheaton College. I had heard he owned his own island in the
Upper Peninsula of Michigan, came from old newspaper money, and only
got paid one dollar a year by Wheaton because he didn't need a salary.
I was a year or so into starting Emmaus and needed financial help, so I
met with Em and asked him point-blank: "I hear you've got some money.
I'm reaching out to men involved in prostitution on the streets and was
wondering if you'd buy me a van?" Em just laughed at me and said, "No."
What he would do, he said, was teach me how to approach people of
wealth and introduce me to his friends called "the Camels."

In the Gospel of Mark we read, "It is easier for a camel to go through
the eye of a needle than for a rich man to enter the kingdom of God"
(10:25). The Camels are a group of businessmen in the western suburbs
of Chicago who came up with their name in light of all their attempts at
getting through the eye of that needle. They tried so many times, they got
bruised. While the group has evolved over the years, the original premise
still drives them: "How do we as wealthy Christian men live justly with the
resources God has given us?"

Carolyn's grandfather, Paul Tobelman, would have liked the Camels. Paul
was the black sheep of his family. While his four older brothers all went
off to the mission field or pastorate, he went into business. During World
War II he started a steel-tubing company and made gobs of money. He
also established college funds for all his nieces, nephews, children, and
grandchildren, and became a major benefactor to the missional work
of his older siblings. Not bad for a black sheep, and definitely eligible
material for Camel status.

The intentionality with which these men approached their wealth was a great inspiration to Carolyn and me when we began to wrestle with what God had blessed us with. When Carolyn and I got married, I brought a bunch of college debt to the table and she brought a healthy chunk of money left over from the college fund that Grandpa Tobelman had set up for her. Fortunately, my debt didn't outweigh her resources, and like many economically blessed young married couples in the mid-1990s, we invested those remaining resources in early Internet stocks. And we made a bundle.

We could have done a number of things with that money. Saved it up for a house in the city or the 'burbs. Traveled to Europe or at least bought a decent large-screen TV. But our "waking up" had already begun.

Carolyn has struggled less than I have with living justly with financial resources. Growing up as a "PK" (Pastor's Kid) gave her an appreciation for frugal living. Her parents' example of welcoming homeless people to dinner and reaching out to the marginalized helped build her sense of justice living. Her background provided us with fertile ground when we started wrestling with the question of "how can we live justly?" with the finances God had given us. The Scripture passage of "where your treasure is, there your heart will be also" (Lk 12:34) convicted us. While our treasure was in a Boston brokerage firm, our heart was in our poor Chicago neighborhood of Uptown, working with these young men on the streets.

Inspired by the Camels, the Scriptures and the Holy Spirit's conviction, Carolyn and I began to pray as we examined our neighborhood's many needs and wondered how we could put our money to use here at home. After much discerning and talking with many friends, we decided to buy a building in the neighborhood.

Our real estate search took us to 921 W. Wilson Avenue. Long known as a crack house and shooting gallery for heroin users, this building was in sorry shape. The wrought-iron front gate was broken and rusting. The front door had been torn off its hinges. While it was mostly abandoned, one family was still inhabiting it and selling crack there. Squatters had been raising dogs on the second floor and fighting them in the basement. The smell of feces, urine, and rats permeated the whole place. In several apartments, person-sized holes in the walls looked like someone had been thrown into the drywall. But despite all that, we discovered the fundamentals like plumbing, electrical, and foundation were in good shape; and that most of the work, with the exception of the roof and needed brick repair, was cosmetic.

Long story short, Carolyn and I bought this building on April 16, 1996. The selling of our stock portfolio gave us enough money for the down payment. We borrowed an additional $40,000 from my parents to pay for needed rehab and then started to run up an additional $50,000 in credit card debt to get the renovations completed before we refinanced. Not the prettiest or cleanest way to rehab a building, but it worked for us.

On a personal level, this building was not just a financial investment. It was a commitment by Carolyn and me to deepen our personal call and investment in God's work in our urban neighborhood. We were committed to the mission of Emmaus Ministries, to our local church, to our neighbors and community, and to "living justly, loving tenderly, and walking humbly with our God" in the midst of the urban chaos around us. We wanted our whole lives, including our pocketbook, to be used by God to do His work in our city. We have committed our all to this task, every ounce of energy we have and every penny in our pocket . . . including some borrowed from our family! We have no regrets.

While Carolyn and I were looking at buildings and trying to figure out what to do as a couple, the Emmaus board of directors and I were also discerning. The directors recognized that the ministry was outgrowing the basement of the rented, single-family home where Carolyn and I also lived.

Over several months the board discussed three options and decided that moving Emmaus to the new building Carolyn and I hoped to purchase seemed to be the best one. The drawbacks to that were examined, too, but after much discussion with our ministry's lawyer and others the board felt that as long as Emmaus rented space from Carolyn and me at or below market value, there wouldn't be a conflict of interest. So about five months after Carolyn and I bought the building, and after the many renovations were completed, Emmaus Ministries moved in.

Over the years, the ministry has taken over various units for its use. The building has six residential apartments (each is 1,400 square feet and features three bedrooms and one-and-a-half baths) as well as a 2,500-square-foot basement. Carolyn and I lived in the third-floor west apartment for the first five years. When our second child was on the way, we moved into a condo in the building behind Emmaus to allow us more space and to separate a bit from the ministry. The apartments that the ministry or our family didn't use were rented out on the open market.

The Emmaus Building, as we've come to know it, has been a great home for this first stage of Emmaus Ministries' growth and development. Not only has the building gone through its own transformation from crack house to ministry center, it has also been a tool of transformation in the lives of our guys.

* * * *

Insurance agents ask the darnedest questions.

Don Holwerda has known me for a while. He was my assistant swim coach in college and has been a faithful supporter of Emmaus since the beginning. This particular afternoon he was visiting our new building to give me an insurance quote. He asked me about the building and my health and then we got on the subject of Emmaus. I shared with him about a few of the guys and how broken they are, and then Don asked something that made me pause.

"Where are these guys' fathers? Some people blame it all on their parents, but that's not the answer is it?"

It was the second part — "but that's not the answer is it?" — that struck a chord.

A few weeks later, after closing on the building, I had hired three guys who were working with me late at night trying to rehab a third-floor unit. Paint fumes tickled our noses as the booming music the guys were listening to pulsated throughout the apartment. The bandanna on my head wasn't doing its job of stopping the sweat from trickling down my face.

Then, above all the racket, I heard the screams.

At first I hesitated, listening closer. In my old Winthrop Street neighborhood drunk folks walking around and arguing late into the night had been a pretty common occurrence. (Many times those loud words woke me from a sound sleep.) I had been finding out it happened even more often on Wilson Avenue.

But then the screams came again with that quality of human panic that sickens your soul.

Moving quickly to the window, I looked down to see a man, probably in his mid-thirties, holding the hair on the back of another person's head. In quick fluid motions, he lifted one knee and brutally slammed into his victim's face. A woman tried to intervene, but the man backhanded her and sent her sprawling. His bloodied first victim stumbled between two parked cars, almost into the path of a passing bus. As the bus went by I realized this was a woman. I saw the blood running from her face was quickly soaking her blouse, and then she staggered quickly down the street and out of view. I looked back to the man and what I saw burned in me. As he turned around, I saw a smile on his face. Then he began to swagger down the street, chest puffed out, fists clenched . . . and that damn smile on his face.

A few days after this, I was meeting with Don again and I shared what had happened. His first reaction — a comment about how the attacker should be shot — echoed the rage I felt. But then once more, Don said, "But that's not the answer is it?"

No, it isn't. But the question sure made me ask, "Lord, what is the answer?"

A week later, Richie, one of our guys, came up to me as I was outside the Emmaus building putting the trash cans out for the weekly city pickup.

Obviously exited, he said, "I was walking over to the McDonald's to get something to eat and I ran into this girl named Michele. We used to prostitute and get high together, and generally watch each other's back. I stood there and stared at her, and when she told me, 'Why don't you take a picture or something!' I realized she didn't recognize who I was. Then I said, 'Why don't you give me a hug? It's Richie.' Her eyes widened and she burst into tears.

"She went on and on about how good I looked, just coming home from work and everything. I told her about Emmaus and how I got off the streets and let God into my life. I also told her she looked like crap."

"I bought her some food, let her come to my place and clean up. I prayed with her and told her I would always be here for her, and so would God."

* * * *

When Richie told me this story I knew the Lord had answered my question. At least partly. I'm not one to think that our city's deep problems that often surface in street violence can be solved quickly and easily. Nothing this complicated has only one cause. Not smoking, not war, not child abuse, not some pimp beating his woman on the street. There are emotional, societal, mental, spiritual, and a host of other factors that lead to the things we do. But at the center of this violence in our world and on our streets are flesh-and-blood individuals. And those individuals can be touched and transformed by the hand of God.

Richie is a testimony to God's transforming power. I could spend years talking with some man or woman on the street with little effect. Richie can stand before them and show them in a powerful way that life doesn't have to be that cold or painful.

That's the result of our process of "waking up" and the inspiration Carolyn and I got from the Camels, Grandpa Tobelman, and the Scriptures: use the resources God has given you justly. For us this meant buying a crack house and turning it into something beautiful for God. Over the years, we have watched as 921 W. Wilson became a vehicle for God's grace to transform lives that in turn will transform the lives of others.

Listen and Reflect

Carolyn's song "The Hard Thing" speaks about the risk of following God's call. Buying this building was a huge risk for us, one that we have never regretted. Listen to this song and consider how it speaks to the risks God might be asking of you. Visit www.greenchoby.com/music-21.html to hear "The Hard Thing."

Read and Reflect

"But those who want to be rich fall into temptation and are trapped by many senseless and harmful desires that plunge people into ruin and destruction. For the love of money is a root of all kinds of evil, and in their eagerness to be rich some have wandered away from the faith and pierced themselves with many pains" (1 Tm 6:9-10).

For Discussion

In his song "Waking Up," Peter Mayer writes, "but I got a nagging notion that enough did not exist."

1. Is he right or wrong?

2. Does "enough" exist?

3. Do you consider yourself wealthy? Go to www.globalrichlist.com and see where your annual income ranks among the people of the world.

4. Are there ways that you can live more justly with the wealth God has given you?

Pray

"O God, to those who have hunger give bread; and to those who have bread give the hunger for justice." (A common prayer from Latin America)

Chapter 9

Street Beating

People often ask me what they should do when they meet a homeless person on the street. I'm a firm believer that the last thing you should do is give somebody money. A handout rarely helps. It might be the easiest thing, but it is seldom the most helpful or most loving.

What people on the street need is your time, touch, or talk. Street people hardly ever get paid any serious attention by the rest of society. They're often overlooked and disregarded. Whether due to our fear or our business, we simply don't take time for them.

Yet a few minutes can go a long way. Street people need others to invest in getting to know them as people and not as objects that can be disregarded. Being homeless and on the street can be very dehumanizing.

No wonder it affects a person's self-esteem.

I found that it also helps to give street people some kind of a healthy touch. A shake of the hand, a slap on the shoulder, or some other simple touch can go a long way to making a person feel more human and appreciated.

Finally, I recommend sincere talk — not *at* them or *to* them but *with* them. A personal conversation can be incredibly healing.

These three T's — Time, Touch and Talk — are the main ingredients to a key principle that I try to live by: "I will do the most loving thing I can for people I meet." Sometimes that's easy, but more often it's very hard.

* * * *

For the third time in a week Shawn came by our ministry high and on the very edge of being out of control. I finally had to tell him he couldn't stop in anymore unless he was serious about getting clean and sober. He left and didn't return for a few days. Then he showed up at our door bleeding from a head wound.

"I got jumped at the crack house down the street, John. I know you said I can't come by, but I just want to get cleaned up, and then I'll be on my way." A nasty cut across his forehead steadily dripped blood down his face and onto his shirt. He was having trouble looking out of his right eye since the blood was streaming over it.

"Shawn, do you want to stop using and get into a detox?" I asked.

"No, I just want to get cleaned up and I'll be out of your way."

"I'm sorry, Shawn. I can't help you." With that I shut the door in his face. Spur-of-the-moment judgment calls like that hold my gut in a vice. But my instincts told me that the most loving thing I could do for Shawn was to show him a clear, consistent, tough love.

Fortunately, it worked. Shawn staggered down several blocks to the local hospital emergency room and got cleaned up. As the doctors stitched up his forehead, he was shocked to realize — through the drug-induced haze of his mind — that I had closed the door on him. God used that experience and several others to wake him up to the dangerous road he was stumbling down.

Shawn started making changes. He went into detox and stayed there for about three months. Carolyn, the other staff, and I visited him in rehab and continued to support him when he went into a halfway house.

During Shawn's first couple of years of recovery, he and I spent a lot of time together talking about his life and helping him navigate the social service systems that were providing him help. His illiteracy was a challenge. (A severe learning disability, lack of parental support, and abysmal poverty had kept Shawn' schooling from going beyond the fourth grade.) At one point, a housing program we helped line up for him fell through, putting him at risk for going back to the streets. After some discussion, Carolyn and I invited him to live with us in our apartment until things worked out. He stayed with us for more than a year and I hired him to help me renovate the 921 W. Wilson building after we bought it. He became a good friend to all of us at Emmaus and something of an adopted "uncle" to our kids when they came along.

And then . . .

After a couple of years of being clean and sober, Shawn relapsed for various reasons and went back to using drugs and prostituting on the streets. In my experience, it seems to take men in prostitution an average of three to five attempts before they make it off the streets. For some it takes longer. Unfortunately, a lot of them never make it. Death, prison, or mental health institutionalization is all too frequently the end for the guys we work with.

Ashamed that he had relapsed, Shawn avoided coming by the ministry center and turned away from any Emmaus staff or volunteers when he saw us on the streets. I was really glad when he finally did stop by for a visit, but he was still getting high and wouldn't quit. On top of that, I had to confront him about taking some the center's recently donated food without asking, and that was when his temper flared.

The clenched fist he shook at me was crusty and dry from many nights on the streets. His light-brown eyes were sunken and yellowed from drug use. I knew that his anger, while vented at me, was really aimed at himself. That was when I found myself making another "tough love" decision.

Even as I ushered Shawn out of the center, the walls bore witness to the hard work he had done when we were rehabbing the building. During that time he had stayed clean, and while he wasn't the best painter in the world, he had hung in there and done most of the interior walls. I had employed him almost full time for a couple of months.

It was hard kicking him out, and I was shaken by his anger and violence.

And that was the beginning of my day.

The afternoon and evening went well. About ten guys came through the ministry center after Shawn. Six of them stayed for dinner, talking with Carolyn, our volunteers, and me across our long, wooden and spread-out dinner table. Afterward we had a wonderful time of worship that included singing, guitar playing, and prayer.

After the guys left, Carolyn and I cleaned up the center and climbed to our third-floor apartment to relax. I asked if she wanted to go to a coffeehouse down the street for some tea. Knowing I needed the break, she agreed and we put on our coats.

At 8 p.m. the streets were dark and a light rain was falling. When we left our building the wrought-iron gate slammed shut behind us. I heard people yelling up the street.

We walked up the block and I saw a man and a woman arguing. The woman was against the building on my left. The man held her arm tightly, pulling her along.

"Get the hell off me!" she screamed and broke free. When he came at her again she swung and hit him hard across the face.

By now, Carolyn and I were only a few feet away from them.

"Hey! Come on, you guys, stop it," I said feebly, attempting to get between the two. Carolyn went over to the woman and tried to help. She shrugged Carolyn off and then moved toward the street, stumbled on the curb, and fell to one knee beside a parked car.

Before we can do anything, the man moved in. In quick succession, he punched her in the face once, twice, three times.

Grabbing the man from behind in a bear hug, I pulled him off the woman and pushed him away. "Stay out of my business man!" he yelled in my face.

"You don't beat a woman on the street!" I screamed back in my nastiest voice, the one I reserve for situations like this. (Not that you should ever beat someone at anytime, of course, but it was all I could think to say!)

Swearing the whole time, he backed off and started stumbling down the street.

"Come with us," Carolyn said, her arm around the woman. "We'll get you some help."

"I don't want no help!" the woman shot back. "I want to go with my man!"

She shook Carolyn off and started down the street after the guy. Not knowing what to do, we turned and walked to the corner. "It's times like this I'm glad you're a big guy," Carolyn said, looking back over her shoulder.

We flagged down a passing squad car and I pointed to the guy who, by this time, was walking toward us. Apparently, someone had already called the police because all of a sudden three more squad cars pulled up. We watched as officers put the man and woman up against the wall. With nothing more to do there, Carolyn and I walked on.

It was clear to us that the couple was high on something, but the fact that the woman ran after her man was disturbing.

We made it to our coffeehouse, ordered some tea, and tried to put the day behind us and relax. Afterward, we stopped by a friend's apartment to say hello. Staying longer than we should have — it was about 10:30 p.m. by then — we left and discovered that the rain had gotten worse. A fierce wind blew rain against us as we walked briskly toward home.

The passing cars made a swooshing sound as they cut through the water on the road. My hood was tight around my face. The rain beat a staccato rhythm on my jacket as I leaned into the wind.

A few blocks from Wilson Avenue someone passed us and Carolyn stopped. "Wasn't that the woman we saw earlier?" she asked. We looked behind us. It was. That wasn't all. About twenty feet in front of us was the man, standing with his back to us.

We walked quickly ahead, trying to pass by unnoticed. I glanced around. The streets were dark and abandoned. The stormy night made everything colder and shadow-filled. This was not good. As we approached him, a lump started growing in my throat. Here was a brutal man whom I had grabbed.

I hate resorting to that on the street. I usually try to de-escalate those kinds of situations with humor and other verbal means, but I had felt I had had no choice with him. Even so, anytime you grab or touch someone on the street without his or her permission, you're committing yourself to a possible physical resolution. And you never know when your guardian angel is on a coffee break.

"This," I said again under my breath, "is not good."

Just as I thought we would get by the guy with no trouble, he turned and saw us. He stepped into my path. I stopped and braced myself. Carolyn took a couple of steps back. The man came closer and his arm swung out . . . offering to shake hands.

I reached out and grabbed his hand.

He looked at me and said, "Man, I am so sorry. I really apologize to you." He kept shaking my hand. "I'm not the kind of guy to do a thing like that. I gots a mom and sister, too, and I wouldn't want nobody beatin' them on the street."

Still surprised and not sure where he was going with this, I answered, "Well, I'm not the type of guy to walk past a woman getting beaten on the street."

He kept holding my hand and pumping it up and down.

"Hey, I respect that," he said. "That's right, man. It's this stuff that's making us do this. You know . . . "

Then he went off on some tangent, taking on the arrogant attitude that so many of our guys have. (When confronted with the horrors of their addictions and obsessions, many people don't want to face the hard reality they're living with. "If this," "poor me," "if only" and "yeah, but" are phrases I hear a lot.) I let him continue a while and then interrupted him in mid-sentence.

"Look," I said. "What you need to do is get rid of the stuff that's making you do this. The first step is giving your life to God. Then you need to go get into treatment."

He stopped talking and stopped shaking my hand, but he didn't let go of it.

"You are absolutely right," he said with a small voice. "That's the truth, man. There's no denying it. There's a lot of love in what you just said. You are absolutely right." With that he finally dropped my hand. He passed by us and walked away, shaking his head. Carolyn and I watched him for a few moments and then continued on our way home.

"HEY!"

We turned around and he came back, grabbed my hand for a final shake, and said, "I gots to tell you, man. I *never* heard that kind of love from a guy like you before. That's pure love. God bless you, man."

He turned and left, and Carolyn and I walked home in the rain.

* * * *

There are times when I feel like our presence in this neighborhood — doing this work — doesn't make a bit of difference. Guys like Shawn still relapse in spite of all our efforts, addictions rule the streets, and violence plagues our block.

Yet in the midst of it all God lets His light shine through.

I'm not sure what that man meant when he said "a guy like you." Perhaps he was only used to people disregarding him and ignoring him. But here was a moment when a bit of time, touch, and talk seemed to get through to him. Neither Shawn nor this street couple is going to be helped by a handout. It's not the most loving thing to do, or to give, to someone on the street. But the "Three T's" can make a big difference.

Digging Deeper

Listen and Reflect

In her last year of college, Carolyn wrote a song called "The Journey Must Go On." It's a simple song that perhaps reflects a scene of the early disciples. Yet the chorus speaks to much of our lives as well: "If we stumble we must keep on walking. If they silence us we'll keep on talking. Because we'll be there before long, my brothers, oh the journey must go on." Listen to it at www.greenchoby.com/music-20.html.

Read and Reflect

This is from Paul's Letter to the Romans: "For the kingdom of God is not food and drink but righteousness and peace and joy in the Holy Spirit. The one who thus serves Christ is acceptable to God and has human approval" (14:17-18).

Catherine de Hueck Doherty founded Madonna House in Canada and lived a life of voluntary poverty rooted in a love for justice. She once said, "There are many ways of praising God. Many ways of prayer to Him. Many ways of searching for Him. Many ways of hungering for Him. But today there is one great way, one deep way, one gentle, tender, compassionate way to assuage this hunger. That is person to person. Make the other aware that we love him! If we do, he will know that God loves him. When he knows that God loves him, he will cease to hunger, for he will know that God has laid a table for him and has invited him to come to His feast, to drink His wine and eat His bread — which is imself."[19]

For Discussion

1. Are there people in your life whom you've taken an "easier road" approach with (such as just giving them some money) rather than the tougher "do the most loving thing" approach?

2. If so, what's stopping you from doing the most loving thing now?

3. When and how can you approach them differently?

4. What will it look like?

5. What would you want to happen differently?

Pray

"God of all righteousness, peace and joy, bring those qualities to our streets and communities plagued by violence and addiction."

Chapter 10

Every time Jesus refers to "my glory" in the Gospels, He is speaking of the cross. When we think of "glory," usually images of an Olympic gold-medal winner, movie star, or rich corporate executive come to mind. It's hard to imagine anything glorifying about crucifixion. Yet Jesus sees glory in suffering, pain, and death. This strange wordplay is only one example of the amazing "reversals" of the kingdom of God described in the Scriptures.

I call them reversals because they are the opposite of how our culture expects us to behave. Here are a few other examples:

— *Honor and recognition vs. humility:* "But this is the one to whom I will look, to the humble and contrite in spirit, who trembles at my word" (Is 66:2).

— *Being first vs. being last:* "'Am I not allowed to do what I choose with what belongs to me? Or are you envious because I am generous?' So the last will be first, and the first will be last."

— *Being happy vs. being joyful:* "Though the fig tree does not blossom, and no fruit is on the vines; though the produce of the olive fails and the fields yield no food; though the flock is cut off from the fold and there is no herd in the stalls, yet I will rejoice in the Lord; I will exult in the God of my salvation" (Hb 3:17-18).

—*Low risk/high return vs. high risk/low return:* "As for me, I am already being poured out as a libation, and the time of my departure has come. I have fought the good fight, I have finished the race, I have kept the faith. From now on there is reserved for me the crown of righteousness, which the Lord, the righteous judge, will give to me on that day, and not only to me but also to all who have longed for his appearing" (2 Tm 4:6-8).

—*Hoarding what you have vs. giving it all away:* "Jesus said to him, 'If you wish to be perfect, go, sell your possessions, and give the money to the poor, and you will have treasure in heaven; then come, follow me'" (Mt 19:21).

—*Living selfishly vs. living justly:* And most important, we have the prophet Micah calling us away from living selfishly to living justly. As I said before, answering the question of "How can I live justly?" has meant my adopting an incarnational approach that is summed up well in the Chinese proverb "Go to the people." The ultimate example of this, of course, is the life of Christ. The Lord God, creator of the universe, incarnates himself into the muck and chaos of our humanity. But he does so in such a way, that how He acts, how He views the world around Him, and how He responds to it is a reversal of the way of the world into which He is born.

Living in our neighborhood of Uptown, reaching out to men involved in prostitution, and meeting lots of people on the street has challenged me to live like this. Never more so than when I saw my mother on the streets.

* * * *

"What's my mom doing at the corner of Wilson and Sheridan in Chicago!" was my first thought.

The short stature, the simple dress, the shining gray hair, the quick ease and gracefulness of her movements — at first glance, all of these characteristics screamed "MOM."

But I knew that my mother was three hundred and fifty miles away in the suburbs of Akron, Ohio. Having just spent a three-month sabbatical living with her and my father, I had grown used to her habits. I knew that on this early morning, Mom was probably sitting at the dining-room table sipping her morning coffee, looking through the Akron Beacon Journal newspaper, and wondering when my father was going to get up and take their dog Trooper for his morning walk.

All of these thoughts raced through my head as I approached the woman at the corner of Wilson and Sheridan. Knowing where my mom really was, I forced my mind to reclassify the woman in front of me from "MOM" to "NotMom." But that was proving hard to do. The woman on the corner could have been Mom's twin!

NotMom was waiting for the light to change, her eyes dancing back and forth, looking for a break in the early morning commuter traffic. A bus rumbled by, shaking her small frame. A wind off Lake Michigan came up quickly behind us. A moment later, NotMom's shoulders rose up in response to the chilly breeze. A small trash tornado swirled briefly in front of me.

I wonder if trash tornados are only a Chicago phenomenon? They're the unlikely convergence of trash left on the streets, strong Chicago winds and the "wind-tunnel" effect of tall buildings lined up in a row. Sometimes these little twisters are quite impressive. I've watched some form into swirling funnels fifteen feet tall — newspapers, fast-food wrappers, napkins, paper cups, dirt, and a thousand other pieces of trash dancing back and forth down a sidewalk. Like their larger, dirt-based cousins that plague the Midwest every spring, trash tornados are interesting to watch from a safe distance. But they can be a pain to get caught in, especially if you're not wearing glasses. Fortunately, that trash twister was small, and I just walked through it.

Ahead of me, NotMom and a few other pedestrians were waiting for the light to change. As I arrived at the corner, I stood behind her and took a closer look. The dirt and stains that marked her simple gray dress became apparent. The morning sun lit up the sidewalk in front of her and through her flimsy dress, I saw her sticklike legs and a lack of undergarments. The single sock on her right foot and her dirty, once-white shoes confirmed my conclusion: NotMom is homeless.

The light changed and our cluster of travelers herded across Sheridan Avenue. As we walked past Uptown Baptist Church, I saw NotMom knock on the basement door. A worker from Residents for Effective Shelter Transitions (R.E.S.T.) opened it with a smile and let her in. That was the last I saw of her, but our brief encounter stayed with me as I continued on my way to the "L train" (as our subway system is called in Chicago) and an early morning meeting downtown.

R.E.S.T. is a social service agency for the homeless that runs a nightly women's shelter in the basement of Uptown Baptist, and NotMom was obviously a client. Perhaps she had gone out to the Burger King across the street for a quick bite before gathering her belongings and starting another day on the "tramp trail."

Living in Uptown, I've seen lots of homeless men and women walking the streets. As I stood on the "L" platform waiting for my train, I wondered why NotMom left such a strong impression on my mind.

I thought about how I describe my neighborhood to other people. It has become a mantra of sorts: "I live in one of the most diverse neighborhoods in the country. At our parish school, there are 270 kids who speak 33 different languages. We have 14,000 elderly, 10,000 mentally ill, and around 1,500 homeless people who call our neighborhood home." This description offers plenty of statistics, but no story. To many people, NotMom is simply one of the 1,500 homeless wandering Uptown. But she's also someone's daughter and perhaps a sister or mother.

How convenient and easy it is for us to hang labels on the poor. That kind of distancing enables us to ease our consciences and ignore reality. It's certainly comfortable to speak of the "homeless problem" and the "rise of homelessness." But it's uncomfortable to think of your own mother on the street.

Can you picture your mother sleeping on a mat on the floor of a cold church basement? She's tucked her shoes underneath her head so they won't be stolen during the night. The snoring and smell of forty other sleeping women keeps her awake most of the night and the 6 a.m. wake-up call comes too early. She stands, slips a thin dress over her head, and goes out the door with a few coins she panhandled the night before. An eighty-nine-cent cup of Burger King coffee wakes her up, and the short walk loosens her stiff bones. By 6:30 your mother is in line for the bathroom and shower. A short ten minutes is all she gets to freshen up. A few more minutes in another line brings her a breakfast of oatmeal and leftover bread from the local supermarket. It's a meal she eats almost every day. It's enough.

By 8 o'clock she's "on the trail." Lunch is four hours and nine blocks away at St. Augustine's Church. She sits for a while at the bus stop, trying to keep the early morning commuters from knocking over her shopping bag. It's a large, tough, brown paper bag from the Nike store downtown, with handles and a cool looking "swoosh" on each side. It's also the carrier of all her worldly possessions. Good bags like this last at least a week. She watches the teachers, food service staff, maintenance guys, and other working poor as they wait to pay their buck seventy-five for a ride on the express bus downtown. Across the street, the young graphic designers, CPAs, and marketing professionals hail cabs for the $15.50 ride downtown in their private yellow chariots. She looks at the cars stopped on Sheridan Avenue and watches the bankers, traders, and CEOs jockey for position in their $80,000 BMWs and Lexus SUVs.

She remembers a life long past, perhaps before the onset of mental illness, domestic abuse, or financial tragedy. She remembers being a mother, a daughter, a sister. Now she is just "homeless," a statistic. With a crick in her knee and tug on her bag, she stands and starts toward lunch at "St. Augie's." Another day on the trail.

My encounter with NotMom reminded me of sitting in court with Jim, whose story I told in Chapter One, as he stood trial. You may recall, a state attorney looked at the jury, pointed at Jim, and cried, "You can't trust him! He's just a hustler!" Years later, I remember that attorney's cry. He looked on Jim as nothing more than a piece of trash swirling around the city.

* * * *

Living justly means living the reversals presented in Scripture. It not only changes our vision but also our actions. What if we looked at each homeless woman as a mother or daughter? Or each male street prostitute as a son, brother or father gone astray? Perhaps we downplay the human dignity of these overlooked souls because to do otherwise would be too painful. That's why NotMom made such an impression on me. I realized how unbearable it would be, for me, if my mom were on the streets.

I've never seen NotMom again. I look for her now and then. I don't know what's become of her, but I offer up a prayer for her on occasion. I'm thankful that she helped me deepen my understanding of what it means to live justly in this world.

Digging Deeper

Listen and Reflect

A couple of weeks before my birthday, Carolyn asked me what I might want for a present. Not that I'm overly romantic or anything, but I asked her to write a song about me, a love song perhaps. She's written a couple of those (I won't tell you which ones they are, you'll have to figure that out yourself). She said "OK" and went to work.

The song she came up with is "Charlemagne," which tells the story of this tenth-century emperor and his funeral. It's a compelling song that speaks well to the "reversals" of the kingdom of God. How it is a song about me, let alone a "love song," I have no idea. But it's still good. Listen to it at www. greenchoby.com/music-33.html.

Read and Reflect

In his *Meditations and Devotions*, Blessed John Henry Newman said:

> God has created me to do some definite service; He has committed some work to me which He has not committed to another. I have my mission — I may never know it in this life, but I shall be told it in the next. I am a link in a chain, a bond of connection between persons. He has not created me for naught. I shall do good. I shall do His work. I shall be an angel of peace, a preacher of truth in my own place while not intending it — if I do but keep His Commandments. Whatever, wherever I am, I can never be thrown away. If I am in sickness, my sickness may serve Him; in perplexity, my perplexity may serve Him; if I am in sorrow, my sorrow may serve Him. He does nothing in vain. He knows what He is about. He may take away my friends, He may throw me among strangers, He may make me feel desolate, make my spirits sink, hide my future from me — still He knows what He is about. Therefore I will trust Him.[20]

For Discussion

Living the reversals can often mean stepping into the unknown. Trust in God can be hard in times of darkness and suffering.

1. At what time has your trust in God been challenged?

2. How did you find your way through?

3. What "reversal" gave you hope or meaning?

4. What in this world holds more power over you than you wish?

Pray

"Just One, Righteous One, help us your children live incarnationally in this world with an attitude of trust and a thirst for justice."

Section III

How Do I Show Mercy?

He has showed you, O man, what is good.
And what does the LORD require of you?
To act justly
and to love mercy
and to walk humbly with your God.

—Micah 6:8, NIV

There is a painting on the wall of the Emmaus Ministry Center dining room. In rich, deep, and vibrant colors, this eight-by-twelve-foot mural shows a depiction of the Last Supper. Every face at the table is African-American. A few years ago some Taylor University art students on spring break asked to sleep on the floor. In return for our letting them crash with us, they left us this mural. When it first went up, many guys in the ministry reacted by saying, "Hold on. Jesus wasn't no black man!"

My response was, "True. But he wasn't a white European either. In fact, he probably looked more like Osama Bin Ladin than Tony Blair." But beyond the artistic license of skin color, what a picture of mercy the mural portrays: Jesus giving himself for proud men like Peter who would deny, Thomas who would doubt, and Judas who would betray. Not only did He incarnate Himself and live among them, He welcomed them to His table.

For me, "loving mercy" has been the exercise and practice of welcoming prodigal sons to my table. This is difficult to do. Narratives, assumptions, and prejudices in our society often form our thinking about ourselves and others, and they can sometimes build barriers between us and the poor. The practice of "loving mercy" means breaking through these narratives and opening our table.

Most people are repulsed by prostitutes, and even a beggar holding a cardboard sign at the end of a highway exit ramp can elicit our disgust. Our attitudes toward the poor and homeless often reflect deeper fears within ourselves. "There but for the grace of God go I" can be a scary thought. We live in a culture with very deep narratives that inform our thinking about others.

Picture any cowboy movie of the last century and you'll see the image of a rugged individual struggling against the odds to overcome hardship. This and other narratives embedded within the American psyche can callous our hearts toward the poor.

We've all heard the phrase "pull yourself up by your bootstraps." It's deeply woven into our culture, but no one really knows its origin. It presumes that we're all are wearing boots, that all our laces are equally strong, and that we each have the strength and ability to pull ourselves up. So when we see people — apparently — not tugging on those bootstraps as we think they should, our hearts harden toward them.

The reality is that life is not a level playing field. The iconic cowboy is a myth, and not all "bootstraps" are equal.

When I first started Emmaus, I realized how naively I had assumed that everyone could get off the streets if they just *tried* a little harder. They needed to be strong, tough, and . . . well . . . just "pull themselves up by their bootstraps"! But what really needed strengthening was mercy within my own heart.

Mercy is like a muscle. It has to be worked, stretched, and challenged if it is to grow.

Dominican Sister Mary Alice Hannon ran a shelter in New York City where I once served as a volunteer. During one of our training sessions she said, "If you look at a street person and are repulsed by what you see, it shows something equally repulsive inside of you." Her words were like a punch in my gut. I knew my attitude needed adjusting. My "mercy muscle" needed some exercise.

* * * *

I expected many things when I took three guys from the streets up to the north woods of Wisconsin for a week of winter camp: brisk, fresh air; the joy of the wilderness; snowball fights; and sledding. What I didn't expect was my "mercy muscle" being stretched.

I watched them from the fence. The foot of snow on the ground was blowing through the barnyard, whirling about my feet. This is how snow is supposed to fall — in light fluffy flakes through tall, whispering pines trees onto a stable.

My attention was focused on Ricky. He, Shorty, and Louis are young men involved in prostitution on the streets of Chicago. On this visit, I was watching Ricky chase an ornery old burro around the yard. With the help of one of the "wranglers," he got hold of the thing, hopped up on it, and was tossed (laughing and yelling) into the snow — all in about three seconds.

Then it was Shorty's turn.

Throughout the weekend, the trio rode horses, bucked burros, cleaned stables, pitched hay, sat around campfires, ate good food, played wallyball, and went snow tubing. It was fantastic.

But it was a hard weekend as well. These guys are America's "poorest of the poor." They have no family to speak of, little education, no discipline, and hardly any work history. They make their money selling themselves on the streets. They sleep in alleyways. Since they're over eighteen and not considered "youth," their only options for places to go are men's shelters and rescue missions.

Their mother is survival and their father is the streets.

In an article in the American Journal of Community Psychology, Dr. Norra Macready wrote, "Most prostitutes have histories of childhood abuse, including sexual abuse, as well as more recent accounts of homelessness, alcoholism and drug misuse. Many suffer from Post-traumatic Stress Disorder (PTSD) caused by the nature of their work." [21] PTSD is an anxiety disorder that can develop after exposure to a terrifying event. Symptoms of PTSD may include flashback episodes, survivor guilt, and a sense of having no future.

These three guys in the early twenties could have been poster children for Dr. Macready. The abuse and neglect that they had already survived in their short lives was horrific. But for one weekend, despite all the trauma of their past, I saw the children in them come out. They might be "young adults," but they seemed like junior high schoolers the way they carried on.

On our last night, we were exhausted and lounged around the fireplace. Ricky came up to me and said, "John, we just wanted to say thanks for all you've done for us."

"Why do you think I do what I do, Ricky?"

"Because you love us and want us to get off these streets and want us to know that God loves us too." After that, we had a great talk about what it means to live your life for Jesus. We talked about what they needed to do to get off the streets, how they needed to change, and what they might have to give up. Conversations like these are moments of grace, and very precious.

The next morning as we were packing up the car to leave, the guys were quiet. They didn't want to go. We didn't talk much on the six-hour drive back to Chicago. Ricky stared out the window and Shorty and Louis nodded in and out of sleep.

As we approached the city, I asked where they wanted to be dropped off. I hoped it would be a friend's house or maybe a shelter. Shorty said, "Take us to our spot!" I wasn't sure what he meant but decided to follow his lead.

His directions took us along the Kennedy Expressway into downtown Chicago. We exited onto Congress Parkway and headed into the heart of the "Loop," the central part of Chicago's downtown. As we passed the Auditorium Theater where shows like *Les Miserables* and *Showboat* are performed, we turned left onto Michigan Avenue and then quickly turned left again onto Van Buren.

Then Shorty directed me to turn into an alley that leads to the back of the Auditorium Theater. At this point, warning bells started ringing in my head. It was late at night. I was in a deserted alley in downtown Chicago. It was three street guys and one kindhearted street minister. This might not be good.

The one-lane alley was filled with melting snow and potholes. As we slowly drove deeper into this concrete canyon, my headlights shone on an industrial-sized garbage can that was bursting at its metal seams. Halfway down the alley we came to "the spot."

At the edge of the wall to my right, a couple feet above ground level, three large heating vents belched warm air into the cold night. The air had circulated through the Auditorium Theater, warming men and women as they enjoyed the elaborate musicals. It eventually was exhausted out into this alley. Flattened cardboard boxes made up the guys' "mattresses" in front of the vents. This was the elusive "spot" I had heard so much about.

As Ricky, Shorty, and Louis piled out of my car, they grabbed their bags and waved, thanking me for a great week at camp. Shorty went to the industrial trashcan and pulled out a blanket he had stashed there. Louis and Rick grabbed some pallets that had fallen down. They propped the pallets up near the vents and "mattresses," creating little wooden tents with enough space to crawl into and, hopefully, be warm.

We talked a bit after they finished and then I hugged them goodbye.

As I backed out of the alley, snow began to fall in light, fluffy flakes. It descended through the urban canyon and melted quickly on the pavement. Through the dancing snow in the beam of my headlights, I saw Shorty laying down his puppy-eyed face onto a mattress of cardboard.

I drove a few miles away and returned to my "spot": a comfortable, heated apartment and a warm bed. All I could think about were those three young men sleeping on cardboard in an alleyway a few miles from where I live.

I took these guys up to the north woods to offer them a taste of a different life, to challenge them to "pull themselves up by their bootstraps" and get off the streets. But instead, I was confronted by my own attitude and heart toward them. I realized that they were survivors and that they were looking out for one another despite the incredible abuse and neglect of their past. They were hoping for a better future. What right did I have to judge them as a person born and raised in comfort and security?

As I lay there on my soft mattress in my heated apartment, I felt the muscle of mercy being stretched till it almost broke. I wept for Ricky, Shorty, and Louis. And for myself.

* * * *

Life is not fair. Some of us are born into indescribable poverty and others into unimaginable wealth. Some of us are born with a propensity to anger or addiction and others never face those challenges. Some of us are smarter than others. Some have more drive, initiative, and vision than we know what to do with, and others are such dreamers that we can't change a tire.

What's false about the rugged individual narrative is that we aren't born into a world of one person. We're born into community. For those who are broken, fragmented, and at times hostile, there's still the rich possibility of becoming part of a community and not living alone.

If mercy within our hearts can be stretched and grow, then perhaps that repulsive part within us will make way for God's grace, forgiveness, and love. Often, that change — that painful growth — starts with changing our attitude toward those who are most wounded by our society.

Digging Deeper

Listen and Reflect

Listen to "Doesn't Mean Anything" at www.greenchoby.com/music-45.html. Carolyn wrote this after a record label wanted to sign her. She didn't sign because the demands of being a traveling singer/songwriter would have taken her away from our ministry and guys like Ricky, Shorty, and Louis.

Read and Reflect

"Speak out for those who cannot speak, for the rights of all the destitute. Speak out, judge righteously, defend the rights of the poor and needy" (Prv 31:8-9; see also Mk 10:21-22; Lk 14:13-14; Rom 12:13; 2 Cor 8:7,9).

For Discussion

Dorothy Day founded the Catholic Worker Movement, a grassroots network of over one hundred eighty-five communities committed to nonviolence, voluntary poverty, prayer, and hospitality to the homeless. In her book titled *Loaves and Fishes*, she wrote:

> A woman with cancer of the face was begging, and when I gave her money she tried to kiss my hand. The only thing I could do was to kiss her dirty old face with the gaping hole in it. . . . It sounds like a heroic deed, but it was not. What we avert our eyes from today can be borne tomorrow when we have learned a little more about love.[22]

1. Would you have kissed this woman?

2. What would you have done in that alley?

Pray

"God of the lost sheep, have mercy on all those who have been led astray, abandoned or can't find their way home. Send your angels to guide them to the Shepherd and into fields of relentless tenderness, mercy, and grace."

Chapter 12

"Bang for Your Buck" Ministry

The word "grace" came to mind one day when I was having a phone conversation with one of our supporters. The father of a good friend of mine, this retired orthodontist helped us out us with a small financial gift each year but wasn't interested in giving more. I asked him why.

"I like to get the most 'bang for my buck' when I give," he said, "and I just don't see the numbers coming from all your efforts. You're a fine young man. I don't want to see you waste your gifts and talents."

His words are ones I hear often, especially when I speak about our work. Other words I've heard include: "They've made their bed. Let 'em lie in it,. "AIDS is the consequence of their sin." And, "Why don't they just get a job?"

The good orthodontist on the phone continued: "These guys you work with seem to be falling back into the streets all the time. I just don't see the successes in your newsletters. It seems like you're wasting your time with a lot of them."

You know what? He's absolutely right.

In the world's eyes, our guys are prostitutes, drug addicts, petty thieves (that's why our annual budget has a line item of one thousand dollars for "theft replacement!"), liars, and manipulators. Many are HIV positive or have full-blown AIDS and still engage in sexual activity. Of the five hundred or so guys we know on the streets and at the Emmaus Ministry Center, the vast majority don't make it despite our best efforts. We see only a handful each year who make a clean break from their addictions, prostitution, and homelessness.

Only a handful.

Is that a big "bang for your buck"?

Nope.

Is that a cost-effective use of resources, finances, and personnel?

Not in this world's terms.

In those terms, are these guys deserving of the time, energy, love, care, and concern we pour out on them?

Not one bit.

When I think about why we do what we do, "grace" is the word that comes to mind, because "grace" is about giving everybody a chance. Even a second, third, and fourth chance if need be.

I can tell you about guys who have made dramatic changes from the streets as a result of our work. I talk with them, get calls from them, encourage them, and am encouraged by them. I can tell you about the incredible "divine appointments" that God has set up on the streets. The hustler we meet who's out on the streets for the first time. The cook in the gyro shop whose father has just died and needs to talk about it. The bartender who just found out he's HIV positive and wants to talk about God, heaven, and all those things he's turned his back on.

But when you look at the work in terms of numbers, "success stories," and pure economics, Emmaus Ministries is not a good "bang for your buck." If that's what you want to support, you probably don't want to send us your money.

That's the hard-truth side of things. And if *only* truth "came through Jesus Christ," as the apostle John wrote (Jn 1:17), then the work of Emmaus would be a waste of time. But the apostle says that "grace *and* truth" come to us through Christ.

* * * *

"Artful Eddie" started out as a small-time lawyer in St. Louis. In 1909, he entered into a partnership with an inventor who created a mechanical rabbit for use at dog tracks. As dog racing was still in its early years, this invention caught on quickly. In 1927 the inventor died, and Artful Eddie used his cunning legal skills to cheat the inventor's wife out of the patent rights. He gained total control over the mechanical rabbit.

Pockets bursting with money, he dumped his wife and took his three kids, including his son, Butch, to Chicago. Like everyone who met the fast-talking young lawyer, Al Capone took an immediate liking to Eddie and set him up at a Chicago dog track.

Dog racing was illegal in Illinois, but by tying up the courts with legal challenges for years, Eddie kept the park open. He didn't stop there though. He used his talents to expand the Capone empire into dog tracks around the country, tax-dodging real estate deals, sham corporations, and political bribes.

While failing as an upstanding citizen, Artful Eddie seemed to be a decent father. As Butch grew, Eddie realized that the life of crime he was living would severely limit his son's chance for something better, so he made a fateful decision: he would turn Al Capone over to the law.

At the trial, a cop pulled Eddie aside and asked him what compelled him to betray Capone. Eddie simply said, "I wanted to give my son a chance."

Capone may have been locked away for good, but the mob did not forget.

A couple of years later, as Artful Eddie pulled up to the corner of Ogden and Rockwell in Chicago, two shotgun blasts ended his life. Inside his coat pocket there was a rosary, a crucifix, a religious medallion, and a poem clipped from the newspaper. It read:

The clock of life is wound but once,
And no man has the power,
To tell just when the hands will stop,
At late or early hour.

Now is the only time you own.
Live, love, toil with a will.
Place no faith in time.
For the clock may soon be still.

Because of his father's sacrifice and the clearing of his family's name, Butch was able to gain entrance to the United States Naval Academy. He graduated with honors and became a naval pilot.

When war was declared with Japan, Butch found himself flying a single-engine Grumman F4F Hellcat fighter over the Gilbert Islands in the Pacific. One day on a mission, Butch and his wingman in another Hellcat spotted nine Japanese twin-engine bombers zeroing in on the aircraft carrier *Lexington*. The pair formed up to attack, but the second Hellcat's weapons jammed, leaving only Butch between the airborne attackers and the 2,100 men on the USS *Lexington*.

Butch attacked the greater enemy force head-on and alone, flying straight into their formation with guns blazing. One by one, he picked off the enemy bombers, downing five of the original nine attackers. Three more were shot down by *Lexington* pilots who were able to take off because of Butch's heroic engagement. The last Japanese bomber, badly damaged in the shootout with Butch, crashed at sea miles away.

Butch's heroism was quickly recognized. He became the first naval aviator of World War II to be personally awarded the Medal of Honor by President Franklin D. Roosevelt, who called his performance "one of the most daring, if not THE most daring, single action in the history of combat aviation." Several years later, Butch's Hellcat was shot down and he was lost at sea.

But that's not the end of the story. Hardly a day goes without a lot of Chicagoans — and many others — saying or hearing his name or visiting his namesake. That's so because after the war, the citizens of Chicago named their new airport after their fallen son: Butch O'Hare.

* * * *

I love that story!

I read it to some of the guys in our ministry center one day and was greeted with a chorus of "No ways!" I don't know what they found more unbelievable — that a father would make such a sacrifice for his son, or that someone with a background like Butch's could turn out to be such a hero.

Both of those observations lead me back to the reasons why I do this work: grace and truth.

The truth is that many of the guys who come to Emmaus have never met their fathers, let alone have any significant relationship with them. It's hard to describe the loss and damage that is done in a young boy's life when his father is absent. When we talk with our guys about what life was like for them growing up, they almost always dance around this father-wound. You can see it in their eyes or hear it in the words they mumble when we do something as simple as watch a movie depicting a father interacting with his son.

As I raise my three sons, Jonathan, Daniel and Peter (and my daughter, Claire), my work at Emmaus has become harder. Not because of time pressures and not because I'm concerned about raising kids in the city. It's gotten harder, in part, because I realize how important I am to my children and how much our fatherless guys have lost.

Can anything possibly heal that father-wound?

Yes! But it's not a program, a service, an outreach method, or a well-equipped drop-in center. It's a deep understanding that there is a Father who sacrificed His own Son for them. It's the presence of friends who help them live in the light of this amazing reality and live up to their potential as fathers, friends, and men of faith. This is "grace" giving a guy a second chance.

In Chapter Nine, I wrote about kicking Shawn out of our ministry center. I explained how he got angry and violent; how he cursed me and accused me of all sorts of things. We were ready to call the police to have him removed, and he and I almost came to blows. Not a good day.

Several months after that, I sat with Shawn in our apartment's guestroom. He had been living with Carolyn and me for a couple weeks while he awaited entry into an out-of-state recovery home and had just returned from the Promise Keepers "Stand in the Gap" rally in Washington,

D.C. The months between that horrible day in the ministry center and our inviting him into our home had seen a dramatic change in Shawn. He had been clean for about five months and was finally dealing with some of the sexual identity issues that led him into the streets. After attending the rally, he wanted to get baptized at the local church he'd been attending, and he wanted me to do it. A Catholic deacon baptizing this prodigal son in a Southern Baptist church. Wouldn't that be something?

Did we have to go out on a limb for Shawn and invite him to be our guest in our home? Nope. Did Shawn do anything that deserved the time and attention we were giving him? Nope. But we wanted to give Shawn a second chance.

Grace. Pure, unadulterated, reckless grace. Yes, Shawn is a sinner. He's lived on the streets for the majority of his life. He's done things to other people and had things done to him that I don't even want to think about. The truth is that Shawn probably deserves what he got on the street.

But ours is a faith that says, "Grace and Truth came through Jesus Christ." We can so easily get caught up in the battle over truth. Protestants and Catholics have warred against one another over truth for four hundred years. We've spilled one another's blood. We've burned one another's churches. We've condemned one another's souls to hell. To this day, in places like Northern Ireland and Central America, Catholics and Protestants continue this war. Truth is important, to be sure. But it loses its soul when separated from grace.

Grace is what calls us to forgiveness, reconciliation, and the love of sinners.

Grace is what calls us out onto the streets, hoping to be vehicles of God's grace and love to men involved in prostitution.

Grace is what allows us to love guys who are unlovable in worldly terms.

Grace is why we spend our time, money, and energy proclaiming God's love to a world entrenched in the lies, manipulations, and snares of darkness.

I want to be like Artful Eddie, ready and willing to make a tremendous sacrifice for a lost son by giving him a chance. I want to lift our guys up to the Lord and see the wonder on their faces when they see God's grace being poured out through our meager efforts. I want to fix my eyes on heaven and be filled with the wonder that — despite all we've done, all the sins we've committed — nothing can separate us from God's love.

Not prostitution, not lies, not promiscuity, not hard hearts, not even all the power of this world can separate us from God's love.

It is a privilege to be a vehicle of God's grace to these men on the streets. I'm not interested in getting a good "bang for your buck." I want to be an explosion of grace in the lives of these men on the streets. An explosion that rocks them to their soul and sears through all the grime and dirt of the streets as they live the embrace of a second chance.

Listen and Reflect

Listen to "Grand Rapids" at www.greenchoby.com/music-15.html. The meditative chorus on this song simply says, "Sometimes love is painfully patient." Giving guys like Shawn a second chance isn't easy. Showing grace to those in our lives who may have hurt us in some way can be the most difficult thing we have ever done. It needs a lot of love and a lot of patience.

Read and Reflect

"Now as you excel in everything — in faith, in speech, in knowledge, in utmost eagerness, and in our love for you — so we want you to excel also in this generous undertaking. I do not say this as a command, but I am testing the genuineness of your love against the earnestness of others. For you know the generous act of our Lord Jesus Christ, that though he was rich, yet for your sakes he became poor, so that by his poverty you might become rich" (2 Cor 8:7-9).

How thankful should we be that God did not look for the best "bang for His buck"!

For Discussion

1. What did you learn or experience in reading the story of Butch O'Hare?

2. When was the last time someone gave you a second chance?

3. Why is it hard for our culture to give the poor a break?

Pray

"God of second chances, bestow on us Your grace, so that we might become rich in mercy."

Chapter 13

Mercy Hurts

I awoke from the dream dripping in sweat. It was gay and erotic, visceral and disturbing. When I realized I was safe in my bed at home, I dropped back onto my pillow, my breath coming in short, ragged gasps. I lay there in the early morning hours and awaited the sunrise, not wanting to go back to sleep. I'm a happily married man and homosexuality has never numbered among my struggles, so this nightmare was shocking.

Later in the day, I met with my spiritual director, Martha. She and her husband, David, run a great retreat house in the western suburbs of Chicago. After retiring from farming, they decided to start a retreat center. They have thirty-three acres, a small stream, a guesthouse converted from a garage, and a friendly herd of deer that wanders their property. Both Martha and David are authors as well. She writes poetry and he penned

Pioneer Naturalist of the Plains, a book about his grandfather.

I must have look stressed because soon after we met, Martha asked if I was OK. I told her about my disturbing dream and talked about how tired I was and how difficult the ministry was at the moment. I talked about the late nights on the street immersed in the gay cruising strip where we do our outreach, about the guys at the ministry center needing help, and about my not being able to get through to many of them. She asked if I was praying regularly. "Umm, not really," I answered. Was I reading the Scriptures? "No, you see, I'm real busy with all these guys I'm working with. . . ." Martha tilted her head and looked at me with that penetrating gaze all good spiritual directors probably practice. After some companionable silence she simply said, "You know, John, if you walk through the barnyard of the world, you're gonna get a lot of shit on your feet."

I always felt Martha was at her best when she lapsed into farmer colloquialisms. And this short, pithy life phrase has stuck with me and reminded me of what's true. When my spiritual disciplines weaken, so do my defenses against the "powers and principalities" of darkness. Prayer, reading of Scripture, silence and solitude, godly fellowship, and worship are not quaint, pietistic Christian practice; they are the lifeblood of a holy, missional life. We neglect them at our spiritual peril.

Showing mercy is messy. Sometimes outwardly, sometimes inwardly. After a night of street outreach, I usually stink of cigarette smoke and body odor. This is corrected quickly by showering and changing clothes. But the inward "shit" has been the hardest to clean up.

Like the painful emotions that come from listening to a young man tell me how a neighbor raped him as a child. Not once, but repeatedly abusing the boy, confusing him sexually and emotionally, and infecting him with various STDs, all before the youth turned fifteen. It's hard to hear that.

Like gut-wrenching anger at seeing guys get into cars to turn a trick and knowing how it was hurting them emotionally, physically, and spiritually. Watching guys with such potential and natural ability fall back to the streets time and again gets tiring. It weighs on your soul and drains your spirit.

* * * *

When I walked into the sterile, shared room at Chicago's Cook County Hospital, the boy lying in the bed next to the door didn't stir. In the bed next to him, through the thin curtain, I heard an Asian couple talking in a language I can't understand and *All My Children* blaring from a television set hanging from the ceiling.

I could see where the bullet was lodged behind Mikey's left ear. The bone seemed to be pressing against the skin as if it was trying to escape. His left eye was hideously swollen; only a tiny black line betrayed his eyelashes amid the red, blue, and black swelling. The lashes contrasted sharply with his pale, white skin. His red hair and freckled face showed his Irish ancestry. Some Irish saint had to be watching out for him.

"You can wake him," the nurse entering the room said.

"No, let him sleep."

"Mikey! Wake up! You have a visitor." Nice bedside manner.

He stirred. "Hey."

"Do you know who I am?" I asked.

"Yeah, I know you. How're you doing?"

"'How are *you* doing?' is the important question here."

"The doctors want to take the bullet out tomorrow. It went in here and is stuck here." His finger pointed to a hole in the top of his forehead, a little above his hairline and left of center. Somehow, someway, a small-caliber bullet fired at point blank range entered his head, skidded along the inside of his skull and lodged behind his ear. All without any severe damage. I stood there amazed at the grace of God.

We talked for a bit. Mikey cried as he told me what happened, but I was sure he didn't tell me everything: A car pulled up, a door flashed open, a "pop" sounded, and Mikey woke up the next day in the hospital. A too-often-repeated scenario in our neighborhood.

I didn't know Mikey's full story. But I did know he wasn't the innocent bystander he tried to tell me he was. He was a crack addict, hustler, and gangbanger. A "hardened" street kid in some people's eyes. He liked to tell people he was twenty-two, but his hospital records showed he was only eighteen.

His mother, who had frantically called me the night before, had that same kind of "hardenedness." She had spent almost two decades on the street, abusing drugs and selling herself. Now, three years clean, holding down a job and going to church, she wanted a better life for her son.

I told Mikey about the conversation with his mom. He just shrugged. "You know, I have people who ain't gonna let this go unpunished," he said with bravado.

It took me a moment to catch up with this line. A couple of seconds earlier we had been talking about his mother, his getting shot in the head, and the dangers of hustling. Now he was back to the "hardened" street-kid facade. Try as I might, I couldn't get Mikey back to that vulnerable child in the hospital, worried about where his life was going. I left the room very afraid for him. If a bullet in the head wouldn't wake him up to the dangers of the street life, what would?

That was the beginning of my friendship with Mikey. I had tried to reach him on the streets to no avail, but when he saw me standing at his hospital bed, something connected. A couple of years went by with him going in and out of prison, and then he showed up at my apartment.

It was seven o'clock on a Monday morning. I was in the shower. The front doorbell rang, and then Carolyn yelled up to me that one of the guys was here. I groaned. "I told them to come by at ten not seven!" Just as I was about to indulge in a tirade about how tired I was of the constant ministry-related interruptions that I couldn't even take a shower, Carolyn called up again, "John, it's Mikey!"

"You mean 'Hole-in-the-head Mikey'?" I call down.

"Yes, it's him."

I dressed quickly and came downstairs, still toweling my hair. Mikey looked a bit manic and was pacing around our living room.

"Hey Brother John, I know I'm early, but I didn't want to miss the trip. I've been up all night, and I know that if I went to sleep now I'd miss out, so here I am."

I had been hoping he would show up for this camping trip that began today. Nothing I could say or do here in Chicago seemed to be working with him, so I thought a change of venue might make a difference.

I took Mikey with me to rent the mini-van for the trip. Looking closely at him in the car, I saw that his ear was puffed up and swollen where the bullet was still in his head. I asked him about it.

"I'm not going to let them take it out, no *&%# way. Those *&%# doctors want to take my ear off! No way am I going to let that happen."

Still the tough kid in a child's body. I was sure Mikey looked pretty fresh on the streets four years ago, but by now the streets had taken their toll. Besides the bullet in his head, there was also one in his arm. His face bore several scars from various fights, his mouth was sore from herpes, and a small stroke had contorted his face. He wasn't even twenty-one yet.

Four other guys arrived for the trip that morning and we took off for the north woods of Wisconsin.

On Wednesday evening, breathing in the fresh air, we were all talking around the camp's dining room table. Mikey chimed in, "You know, if I could, I'd go live with my gram outside Rockford. She's the only one who's ever loved me. She raised me. But every time I get eleven dollars together for the bus I smoke it up."

"Why don't we drop you off there on the way back to Chicago?" I offered. Mikey looked at me with timid eyes and said softly, "You'd do that?" So on our return trip from the north woods we made a little detour to the farming country of northwestern Illinois. As we entered the little town where Mikey grew up, he became visibly excited.

"Over there's the youth center. . . . Right there's a great spot to catch catfish. . . . I wonder if my friend Janet still works at the store. . . . It's been five years since I been here but it still looks the same." From the mean streets of Chicago via the north woods of Wisconsin, a young man was returning home.

His grandmother was delighted at their reunion. We took a picture of us with her, wished Mikey the best, and headed back to Chicago.

Only a few days later, Mikey paid us a visit after he had had a doctor's appointment. He learned that surgery to remove the bullet could be done without removing his ear and it had been scheduled in a couple of weeks at a hospital near his grandmother's. She also found him a job bagging groceries at the local store where his friend Janet once worked. The best news: he and his mom went to church and he asked God into his life. Mikey stayed with us most of the afternoon and I never heard him swear once.

A year or so went by and Mikey seemed to be doing well. We lost touch a bit and then one day walking through our neighborhood I heard somebody yell from a passing car, "John! Was' up?" I looked at the brand-new Ford Expedition and Mikey waved from the passenger seat. He and another young guy were cruising through our 'hood. I was pretty sure the car was stolen, and I could only shake my head.

A couple months later, Mikey showed up at my door. He had just gotten released from jail. I was unsure of the exact story, but he said something about shooting at a police officer, or helping to steal a car, or his getting arrested for statutory rape of his sixteen-year-old girlfriend, or (according to him) a beating she received from the police . . . . And it went on and on.

I had been on my way to run some errands, so I took Mikey with me. He kept jabbering about how he needed to "beat the case" until I finally told him to stop.

"Mikey, it's not the case or your girlfriend or your using or whatever that I'm interested in. I'm interested in your making a fundamental change in your heart and soul and character; that is the only thing that will keep you from getting killed."

He listened for a while, then said he had to meet some folks and got out at the corner. I watched him walk away and truly felt like I was watching someone who would die very soon.

And there was nothing I could do about it.

Mikey dropped out of sight and I assumed he was dead. Then I got a call from his mom inviting me over for dinner. It was a drive, but I headed out of the city to the small farming town where she lived. Mikey had been out of jail only a couple of weeks after serving three years for prostitution, drug possession, and car theft.

"I know why he does what he does," Mikey's mom, Elaine, said to me as Mikey opened the Christmas presents I brought him. "I was out working the streets all the time he was growing up. He saw me with so many men I can't even imagine what it was like for him. I tried to do my best, but I was caught up in it all. I'm lucky I didn't lose him." Mikey thanked me for the socks, shirts, and other gifts, and then went to get some more coffee.

Elaine continued. "I've been clean and sober for five years now. I got saved in jail and ain't never going back to that life. It's been hard, but I got married a year ago, and Greg is a good man. He's watching out for me and

Mikey's two younger brothers."

"But mom and me have had a tough time," Mikey interjected, setting a second cup of coffee in front of me. "I've been wild ever since I was young. It's all I knew. Now I'm trying to make a better life, but it's hard out here. It's so different from Chicago."

"I almost didn't let him into my home," Elaine said. "I prayed and prayed and asked God what I should do. I didn't want his madness to affect my family. But I realized his madness is mine and I needed to do what I could to help him." And with tears in her eyes and a look that seemed to remember all the times she'd let him down, she added quietly, "And he's my son."

Mikey lasted a couple years with his mom. He worked odd jobs, moved in with his girlfriend, and had a daughter. He has matured in fits and starts, but still gets into trouble.

* * * *

Mikey is one of those guys I've watched for years as he's tried valiantly to get his act together but has fallen short time and again. When I first met him on the streets, he wouldn't talk to me. It took a bullet to the head to get his attention.

I have hurt for Mikey so often. I've walked through the barnyard of his world and gotten a lot of shit on my feet. In this ministry, I am reminded almost daily that "our struggle is not against flesh and blood, but against the powers and principalities of darkness." Those powers seek to destroy our sons, daughters and families. They seek to corrupt, lie, cheat, and steal away our love for one another.

These powers also reared their ugly head in the erotic nightmare I awoke from.

But it's not about me. Two thousand years ago, God did something insane. He entered into our humanity with all its dysfunction, brokenness, and madness. In the fragile form of a babe in a manger, He came to live among us as if to say, "You are not alone. You are my beloved, my family. Be part of me, as I seek to be part of you. Love me. And love those ragged, fragile, hurting ones that I bring to you."

God's insanity redeemed our madness. The darkness is still there. There's a lot of shit on the ground that we have to walk through. But even if it destroys our fragile family here on earth, we know that it will never defeat the infinitely enduring family we have in God.

We are beloved, no matter how wounded, broken, or betrayed we are. We will always be loved.

Listen and Reflect

Carolyn's song "Blood On Their Hands" was written after she heard about a gang-style killing down on the Southside of Chicago and where the young gangbangers ended up. It's a haunting and arresting song. Listen to it at www.greenchoby.com/music-44.html.

Read and Reflect

In *Making All Things New*, Father Henri Nouwen wrote: "Poverty, pain, struggle, anguish, agony, and even inner darkness may continue to be part of our experience. They may even be God's way of purifying us. But life is no longer boring, resentful, depressing, or lonely because we have come to know that everything that happens to us is part of our way to the house of the Father."

For Discussion

1. What is your hope or prayer for Mikey and those like him?

2. Is it difficult to understand Father Nouwen's quote of how struggles are part of the journey?

3. Is the Christian life intended for suffering and difficulty?

Pray

"Teach us, good Lord, to serve Thee as Thou deservest; to give and not to count the cost; to fight and not to heed the wounds; to toil and not to seek for rest; to labor and not to ask for any reward save that of knowing that we do Thy will."

—St. Ignatius of Loyola

Chapter 14

The Prodigal at the Table

If you've met me in person, you know that I haven't missed many dinners. I like to eat. I'm only 5 feet 10 inches tall but I tip the scales at over 250 pounds. I'm the baby of six kids, and as I grew up family dinners were raucous affairs, complete with laughing, teasing, and whines or requests for more helpings. Not only did we get nutritional sustenance, but it was in those times that we connected most as a family. And we ate a lot.

From early on in our ministry, Carolyn and I found that sharing a meal with guys who came by our ministry center was an important time of connection. In the beginning we hosted meals on Wednesday nights. Volunteers often helped with the cooking, and the guys pitched in as well. Now we serve dinner on Wednesdays and Saturdays, and lunch five days a week.

In those early days we never knew how many guys would show up for a meal, so food preparation was a challenge. For a while, having a pot of water boiling gently on a backburner was a good trick. If a lot of guys showed up and the food we had prepared wasn't going to be enough, we would throw some pasta in the water and grab a can of spaghetti sauce from the pantry to supplement our meal. Other times we'd prepare a large meal and only one or two guys would show up, condemning us to eating leftovers for the rest of the week.

After dinner, Carolyn would lead us in praise and worship on the guitar. We never told guys they had to stay for this, but most of the time they did. One night, a young man named Joseph wanted to sing one song, over and over again. I'll never forget that Wednesday evening.

* * * *

As I talked with Joseph in the living room our dog, Mandy, played tug of war with one of the guys. In the dining area, Carolyn, a volunteer, and some of the guys were cooking and setting the long table for the ten or so people present. Over in our small clothing room, another guy was searching the closet for a dress shirt to wear to a job interview the next day. Another guest slouched in a recliner and casually flipped through a magazine as he waited until dinner was ready. The evening sun filtered through the high windows, bouncing off the hardwood floors and creating interesting shadows and rays on the walls. It was a relaxing night and I was at ease.

Joseph was sitting next to me on the couch. I didn't know him that well. One of our outreach teams met him a few days earlier prostituting on the streets. They gave him the Emmaus card and invited him to come by the ministry if he wanted help. He showed up the next day.

Joseph was well built for a guy on the street. His muscles rippled under his T-shirt and he couldn't have had more than five percent body fat. His dark complexion contrasted sharply with the whiteness of his eyes and teeth. He kept his hair short. He seemed nervous this evening, so I thought a little small talk might calm him down. I casually asked him, "How did you hear about us, Joseph?"

"I met these people down on Halsted Street who told me about you guys. I really like it here. It feels good." We chatted a bit more and our conversation drifted to sports. I asked him if he worked out a lot. "Nah, I got this," he said, flexing an impressive bicep, "at Stateville." That answered the fitness question. Stateville is an Illinois penitentiary south of Chicago. Many of our guys who go to prison come out pretty ripped. Not much to do in jail besides play cards and lift weights.

As we chatted, he still seemed nervous but I couldn't tell why. We talked more about the streets and the Cubs, and then drifted into silence. After a few minutes he leaned close to me and spoke in almost a whisper. "You know John, I've never done this before."

I went blank. I couldn't figure out what the heck he meant. I racked my brain, quickly reviewing our conversation, what I knew about him, his body language when he leaned into me, and his whispering. Then I thought, "Oh, no. He thinks I'm a 'trick'. He must think something sexual is gonna happen here." For a couple seconds I didn't know what to do, and finally just said, "Whoa, whoa, what are you talking about?"

Looking around to make sure nobody could hear us, he leaned even closer to me and said, "You know, this family-dinner thing, I've never done this before. But I've seen it on TV."

Then I realized what Joseph meant. The twenty-eight-year-old man sitting next to me had never, in his whole life, sat down around a dining room table and had a family meal. I was shocked. At the time I had had almost a decade of street ministry experience under my belt and didn't think much could catch me off guard. But Joseph's hushed confession took my breath away.

Soon after that we were called to the table, sat down, said our grace, and launched into the meal. Everything went well. Joseph ate heartily and laughed, listened and passed food, his nervousness slowly melting in the companionable warmth of a family dinner.

After we finished, a few guys cleared the table and others washed and dried the dishes. My motto with guys at the ministry has always been, "You walk through the door, you do a chore." No handouts here. It's important that everyone contributes somehow. This is not a soup kitchen.

When all the dishes were done we gathered in the living room for some music. Carolyn tuned her guitar and started us singing. Halfway through this time of worship she sang a song about redemption and hope. When it was over, Joseph suddenly shouted out, "I love that song! Sing it again, sing it again!" and Carolyn dutifully obeyed. In fact, she sang it three more times before Joseph seemed satisfied. Perhaps the lyrics resonated with the longing in his soul. We all prayed together and then the guys went on their way.

Several weeks after that night, I took Joseph and some guys camping. At one point, we returned to our bunkroom to change clothes for dinner. I watched as Joseph removed his dirty shirt, and once again he shocked me. His body was a fleshy tablet upon which his tragic life had been written. Two pockmarked bullet wounds speckled his shoulder blades, a couple of knife wounds had healed in straight but embossed lines across his chest, and a large surgical scar ran up his spine, which had been cracked in a prison fight.

I learned more of Joseph's story on that trip. At the tender age of four months old, abused and neglected, he was taken from his mother and turned over to the less-than-tender mercies of the state child-care system. During the next fourteen years he was shuffled in and out of foster homes and group homes more than eighty times. He spent much of his teens in juvenile detention, and by the time he turned eighteen he was on his own and looking to make his place in the world. With a female prostitute, Joseph fathered a child who was soon taken by the state much the same way he had been. Joseph's own addiction landed him in prison and then a felony conviction sent him to Stateville for several years. Upon release, with no family, no education, and no job history, finding work was hard. One thing led to another and he started prostituting to get by.

When I returned home from that camping trip, I told Carolyn about Joseph's story. Over the next couple of days, she hummed a new tune and at night she plucked on her guitar, her singer/songwriter muse hard at work. A few days later, she invited me to listen to her new song called "Joseph." (There's a link in this chapter's "Digging Deeper" to listen to it online.) Here are some of the lyrics:

> Joseph was a man who was broken before his time, right from the scars on his chest to the crack in his spine. He knew the alleys and the hallways, the crack vials, the colors, the crimes, he knew the cold steel of the bars where he did his time.
>
> Joseph was a man who had never been a child. Never knew the trust of a hug or the Grace of a smile. He had never sat down to the table of a family meal. He was accustomed to being denied the privilege to feel. Joseph had a son who had the shape of his father's eyes. Born from a night of respite in the arms of a lie. His

mother could not be trusted, for the habits she kept, so he was taken away to live with some people he had never met.

Joseph had a friend whom he saw one lonely night. Told him of a house full of friendship, acceptance and light. He entered the house, there, to learn what the people sang, and once he caught on he wanted to sing it again and again.

* * * *

I've lived in many homes. The one I grew up in was your basic suburban house with four bedrooms, two baths, living room, dining room, kitchen, basement, porch, yard, garage, nice parents, good friends . . . the works. It was great.

My home in New York City for two years overlooked Eighth Avenue and the Play Palace porn theater. It took me three months to get used to the sound of the buses at night and other noises from across the street.

For one summer in my early twenties, my home was an orphanage near Antigua, Guatemala, where I was known as "Papá de Tiburón," Father of Jaws. It wasn't a clever reflection on my swimming abilities, but was given to me because there was a young kid there named Tiburón who had a big belly. The day that I walked into the orphanage, another kid looked at me with wide eyes, pointed to my large stomach, and exclaimed in awe, "Papá de Tiburón!" This sent all the other kids into hysterics and me into confusion.

So what is a home?

Somewhere I came across this century-old description from Austrian opera singer Ernestine Schumann-Heink:

> A roof to keep out the rain. Four walls to keep out the wind. Floors to keep out the cold. Yes, but home is more than that. It is the laugh of a baby, the song of a mother, the strength of a father. Warmth of loving hearts, light from happy eyes, kindness, loyalty, comradeship. Home is first school and first church for young ones, where they learn what is right, what is good and what is kind. Where they go for comfort when they are hurt or sick.

Where joy is shared and sorrow eased. Where fathers and mothers are respected and loved. Where children are wanted. Where the simplest food is good enough for kings because it is earned. Where money is not so important as loving kindness. Where even the teakettle sings from happiness. That is home. God bless it.

A sense of home is deeply rooted in all of us. We need it; we crave it. So do our guys. Most of them didn't have much of a home, much less anything close to the one I had or what Schumann-Heink describes. Dr. Donald Allen, in a study in the "Archives of Sexual Behavior," reported that a whopping "eighty-two percent of male prostitutes come from families where the father was absent, alcoholic, or abusive."[23]

Joseph was impacted by our ministry not through what someone told him or taught him or a service he received. He was impacted by who we are — a family, a home, a community. Whatever you want to call it. Joseph needs a lot of help with his life. All our guys do. They need psychiatrists, social workers, drug treatment programs, transitional living programs, social services, and much, much more.

But beyond all these programs and services, our guys need a sense of family and home — a seat around the dinner table where they hear someone say, "Tell me about your day."

The Lord's Supper mural that hangs in our dining room depicts Jesus at a table with His disciples. From the testimony of Scripture, it's obvious they were an unruly bunch. Fishermen, tax collectors, rebels, deniers, doubters, and betrayers. A bunch of prodigal sons to be sure. Jesus welcomed that ragtag group of men to His table. We'd do well to imitate His example by showing mercy to the lost and forgotten of this world, not by creating bigger and better "services" for their issues but simply by inviting them into our homes and welcoming them to our tables.

Digging Deeper

Listen and Reflect

Carolyn's song "Joseph" tells the story of this Wednesday night meal. Listen to it at www.greenchoby.com/music-43.html.

Read and Reflect

"When you give a luncheon or a dinner, do not invite your friends or your brothers or your relatives or rich neighbors, in case they may invite you in return, and you would be repaid. But when you give a banquet, invite the poor, the crippled, the lame, and the blind. And you will be blessed, because they cannot repay you, for you will be repaid at the resurrection of the righteous" (Lk 14:12-14).

In Luke, Jesus describes a couple of images of welcoming the poor to the table. They are metaphors for the Great Feast in heaven. Consider what they have to teach us today.

For Discussion

1. At what "tables" today are the poor welcomed?

2. At what "tables" are they not welcomed?

3. Are there ways you could invite the poor, crippled, lame, or blind to your table?

4. When was the last time that someone who is poor or somehow disenfranchised by our world sat down at your dinner table?

Pray

"Lord of the feast, may the tables of our homes and hearts be places where the poor and outcast are welcomed with joy."

Chapter 15

God's Eyes

One afternoon I was talking with one of our board members, Gene Frost, about why he got involved in Emmaus. We have similar backgrounds. We were both raised in faith-filled homes in comfortable suburbs by loving parents, both graduated from Wheaton College, both had great marriages and wonderful kids. And now both of us were sitting in the Emmaus Ministry Center, devoting our time, talent, and treasure to reaching men involved in prostitution. I asked why he was so invested in this.

"Because this is my tribe," he said. "I think all of us are tribal by nature, and somewhere along the line God is going to put some people, group, mission, or ministry on your heart. You're going to have to choose to follow where that leads, no matter what and no matter the results."

I've never forgotten that conversation. I often refer back to it when asked, "Why do you work with male prostitutes?"

For some reason, still somewhat unknown to me, this is "my tribe." These men who resort to survival sex generate a compassion and response in me like nothing else. I'm concerned about other needs and problems in the world, but I know deep in my heart that ministering to these men is what I'm called to do. Fortunately, other people like this board member feel this call also and do their part.

Our challenge is staying faithful in the midst of disappointment.

* * * *

Jim and his wife, Ellen, sat in the back pew. Our church was celebrating the feast of Corpus Christi, the Body of Christ. At different times each Sunday, four different language congregations gather for worship: Vietnamese, Spanish, English, and Laotian. But on this feast day, we were all together for one multilingual service.

Carolyn and I stood up front with the English choir. Looking over the crowd, I could see Jim holding his five-month-old son, Jim Jr. During the service, I could hear the little one joining in the songs with baby gurgles and chortles.

After church, Jim and his family took the bus back to their apartment. He had told me he was tired and wanted to go home and take a nap.

I smiled.

Jim was tired because he had been working full time for one of our board members who runs a construction firm. Jim's muscles were well-toned from this hard labor, but more importantly, his rent was paid, his family had food on the table, and his son had formula and diapers. Jim was providing for his family.

The previous September, with a faint hint of winter air beginning to blow into Chicago, we found Jim hustling in one of the bars in which we minister. After a couple of months, he started to talk with Marcus, our outreach coordinator at the time.

Growing up in Uptown had not been easy for Jim. He learned to survive by thinking quick, hitting first, and hitting hard. He did time in prison and after that he ended up working one dead-end job after another. When he got married, he found it difficult to provide for his wife and himself. Then Jim learned he was to be a dad. From his rough-and-tumble upbringing, he knew he could count on hustling to pay the rent and put food on the table.

We met Jim while his wife was pregnant. At first, we helped them out a bit. We paid for Lamaze classes for the couple, and after Jim Jr. was born we helped out with food and diapers. Then Jim started working regularly at one of our board member's businesses. As he worked, his self-esteem and confidence rose. A few months later, he started coming to church with my wife and me. The multiethnic celebration of Corpus Christi was a joyous event. Seeing Jim and his family sitting in that pew worshiping the Lord filled my heart with much joy.

Jump ahead six months.

I wish I had God's eyes.

At 1:00 a.m. on Halsted Street, the pale, yellow glow of street lamps is everywhere. I'm walking toward Rounds, one of the local hustler bars where we maintain a presence. The streets are busy.

Police cars pass from the precinct house not two blocks away. Men stumble out of clubs and try to hail cabs through their drunken stupor. Neon lights scream beer advertisements at me as I walk past the bars. A passing bus belches fumes; an old car engine sputters for want of a tuneup.

Standing still, I see a couple of dozen people out and about. Across the street, a few young gangbangers nervously look around. A car pulls up. Movements are liquid quick, practiced many times by boys no more than fourteen or fifteen. Money for the drugs. Drugs for the money.

Two men locked in a lovers' embrace walk by me. Their kisses are passionate and their talk obscene. As they near Rounds, one man contests going in, indicating he is beneath such a sleazy place. The other relents and they continue their strolling embrace.

Another car pulls up. Eyes from inside make contact with a young man on the sidewalk. The driver nods his head and glances toward the empty passenger seat. The young man looks left, then right. He saunters to the car and leans in the passenger window. A moment later, the two drive off. Elapsed time from car pulling up to car driving off: twenty seconds.

That short scene tells me many things. The man in the car is a trick, a client, a "john," a customer to a man in prostitution. The young man is his "date" for the night. The young man, not knowing who this guy was, leaned in the window first before getting in. He immediately scoped the driver out to determine if he was a cop or a crazy. Satisfied that the risk was worth the money he expected to earn, he got in the car with this stranger.

All this and more I see walking one block.

What does God see on Halsted Street?

I wish I knew.

Does He see the ragged cops, tired of arresting the same hustlers and drug dealers night after night? Does He see the fear in the fourteen-year-old gangbanger as he passes drugs to a dazed and stoned crackhead? Does He watch as a man, once caught up in the rush of desire, mourns his lover's death to AIDS? Does He watch where the young man and his "client" go for their "date"?

Continuing down Halsted Street, I'm disappointed to see Jim. He was doing so well. The image of him and his family in church on the feast of Corpus Christi still burns in my mind. But here he is, strung out and prostituting.

A couple weeks earlier, he was sitting in my office. The tension in the air was thick. Jim spoke about his need to get clean, to get into a rehab and deal with his crack addiction. He had lost about twenty pounds in the last couple of months. He had avoided us on the street. But now he was begging for help. You could see the conflict warring within him. It was written on his face. He knew he had to get clean, but a large part of him wanted to continue to get high. We talked about his options. About detox and what that was like; about outpatient and inpatient programs; and most of all about giving your life, addiction and all, over to God.

So now, there was Jim hustling on Halsted.

What does God see when He looks at this man?

As I approach Jim, he saw me and turned the corner. I hurried, but he had already gone. Perhaps he had jumped in a trick's car, ducked into the alley, or just hidden in the shadow of a doorway. Wherever he was, it was clear he didn't want to talk with me.

So I walked away with nothing but a prayer for Jim. But maybe that was enough.

A few days later, I found myself sitting with Jim in a back alley outside of a detox center. It was about six o'clock in the evening. He had been waiting for an open bed since two that afternoon. He was hungry, tired, and seemingly had had enough of the drugs. After that night when he ditched me on the street, he decided to try once again to get help for his addiction. He prayed to God to give him the courage to get clean. He called me up and asked for help. I gave him the address of the detox and told him to head there and I'd meet him. And so I did. What impressed me this time was his determination. With a wife and child waiting for him at home, he knew there was a lot at stake. So he was determined to wait at the door until he could get help.

I've seen a lot of Jim. I've seen him hold his son close and sing the little fellow to sleep. I've seen him at church praying with the congregation. I've seen him walking with drug dealers, a crazed look in his eyes. I've seen him strung out and begging for hope, and now I've seen him determined to get help.

Maybe this is what God sees.

* * * *

Why help these guys when they relapse and fall back so much? Why endure the emotional roller coaster of seeing them in church one month and watching them get into a trick's car the next? Why go through the trouble of sitting in a smelly, rat-infested alley waiting for a detox bed to open with no guarantee that this time it'll work?

Because this is my tribe and this is my calling.

It's dangerous to assume that you'll get "warm fuzzies" for being obedient to God's call on your life. We may be tempted to think that we'll earn that extra crown in heaven. Or perhaps more likely we assume that we'll be rewarded by the improvements we witness in others' lives as a result of our hard work. But any time we enter deeper into a calling on our lives, we can count on sacrifice and struggle. Ultimately, showing mercy means that I walk alongside broken men and invite them to the table of fellowship with Christ. That's what I'm called to be faithful to. The result of my actions, and whether these men join the Bridegroom at the wedding feast in heaven, is between them and God.

Whatever your calling or tribe, you have to ask yourself, "Would I do this ministry if I knew there would be no results?" Time and again, I'm disappointed when men return to their addictions or turn their backs on a good job opportunity. But the fact is that God is in control. He has called me to this work, to do it the best that I can. That's all I can do. If I'm in it for more than that, it's not faith, but simply enlightened self-interest.

Find your tribe, answer your call, and do your best.

Let God take care of the rest.

Listen and Reflect

The song "Hustler" was written almost twenty years ago. In it Carolyn lyrically captures the sights, sounds, and feel of being on outreach on the streets at night. The chorus speaks of our calling to reach these guys. The song can be listened to at www.greenchoby.com/music-30.html.

Read and Reflect

"For I was hungry and you gave me food, I was thirsty and you gave me something to drink, I was a stranger and you welcomed me, I was naked and you gave me clothing, I was sick and you took care of me, I was in prison and you visited me" (Mt 25:35-36).

For Discussion

When I speak to students I'm often asked, "How do I find my tribe?" or "How do I find my calling?" God's ways are not always my ways, and often my spiritual life looks more like a drunk stumbling down an alley than two sets of footprints in the sand. I've found it helpful in those times of confusion or "un-clarity" to opt for God's "default command": serve the poor. Visit a prisoner, feed someone who's hungry, clothe the naked, bind up the brokenhearted, or give a cup of water to the thirsty. Often while doing these corporal works of mercy we find deeper meaning, purpose, and calling on our lives.

1. Who is my tribe?

2. What is my calling?

Pray

"Father of mercy and compassion, give that same mercy to those who call upon your name."

Section IV

How Am I Called to Walking Humbly?

He has showed you, O man, what is good.
And what does the LORD require of you?
To act justly
and to love mercy
and to walk humbly with your God.

— Micah 6:8, NIV

So he told them this parable: "Which one of you, having a hundred sheep and losing one of them, does not leave the ninety-nine in the wilderness and go after the one that is lost until he finds it?" . . .
"Or what woman having ten silver coins, if she loses one of them, does not light a lamp, sweep the house, and search carefully until she finds it?" . . .
"'But while he was still far off, his father saw him and was filled with compassion; he ran and put his arms around him and kissed him'" (Lk 15:4,8,20).

These parables all have the same message: God is active in seeking out and saving that which is lost. For me, walking humbly with God has meant finding those places of the Lord's activity and joining in the fray.

Chapter 16

Scuff Marks on the Sidewalk

I had a "Footprints in the Sand" poster on my bedroom wall when I was in high school. It's a famous poem about God carrying us during difficult times. When it's printed on a poster, the background is sometimes an idyllic beach view, with waves gently lapping the surf under the setting sun and a nice, orderly set of footprints heading down the sand. It's the kind of poster that makes you want to tilt your head to one side and let out a satisfying "Awwww . . ." as you melt into the peaceful image.

It's hard for me to picture my walk with God in those pleasant terms. My walk with Christ has been more like a battlefield than a beach. If I had to rewrite that familiar poem, I'd call it, "Scuff Marks on the Sidewalk." The poster would show a chaotic urban scene: blowing trash, homeless folk sleeping on a bus bench, delivery trucks belching toxic clouds of diesel, bike messengers and SUVs fighting it out, a diverse mix of pedestrians on the stroll, and a bit of blood and vomit splattering the sidewalk. The scuff marks are those times God dragged me — kicking, screaming and digging in my heels — forward in my spiritual life. Or perhaps they mark the times I was so filled with despair that I dropped to my knees in anguished prayer, and God grabbed the back of my shirt collar and towed me onward.

You can read the Micah phrase "walk humbly with your God" and the image of a cloistered monk in a bare, monastic cell might come to mind. Or perhaps a humble, spiritual person having "quiet time" in the wee hours of the morning, reading Scripture from a well-worn Bible in his or her favorite and most comfortable chair. Both of these are lives worth imitating, but these portrayals are centered around the word "humble." On the other hand, during the last twenty years of my street ministry, I haven't been able to forget the words "with God" in that command from Micah. That's so because on the streets God is actively seeking out and saving that which is lost. Those three parables from Luke 15 that begin this section depict God as a shepherd seeking out his lost sheep, as a woman sweeping the floor for her lost coin, and as a father running to meet his wayward son. God is already in action, searching for his beloved sons and daughters.

This final charge from Micah 6:8 calls us not to the monastic cell or comfortable chair, but to humbly grab hold of God's coattails and hang on for dear life. Sometimes the roller-coaster ride of walking with wounded and hurting people can make us drop to our knees and want to give up. That's when I trust God has me in His grip . . . and, if necessary, is dragging me along.

That certainly was the case with Samuel.

Samuel's parents divorced when he was just a baby, and he grew up without even seeing a picture of his father. His mother did her best to raise him, but working three jobs to feed four kids meant she wasn't around much. An older male neighbor introduced a young Samuel to sex; the neighborhood gangs introduced him to drugs and hard liquor; and the poverty of his community introduced him to survival at any cost. By the age of sixteen he was wandering through homeless shelters and living on the streets, prostituting himself to feed his stomach and his habit.

* * * *

Carolyn and I were heading out on a date night and were slowly pulling the car out of the alley next to our Emmaus building when Samuel waved from across the street. His dark skin blended into the building behind him, but his blazing white smile shined like a beacon. He bobbed and weaved his way toward us through the busy evening traffic and reached into the passenger window to give Carolyn a big hug. I stretched over and shook his hand. He looked great. Eyes clean and bright, hair neat and trimmed, and winter jacket new and warm. He was coming by for the Saturday evening meal at our ministry center. As he stood there, leaning into the passenger window, I looked past him to the awning of the building next door and recalled another time that he made his way to Emmaus along this same sidewalk. That time he was naked, high, and bleeding.

On that previous encounter eight years earlier, Samuel was in the apartment building next to Emmaus "turning a trick." At twenty-two, he was an experienced prostitute. A guy had propositioned him on the street and taken him back to his apartment for paid sex. When the "client" brought out a crack pipe and started taking hits, Samuel joined in. Everything had been going "fine" until a knife appeared. I'm not sure of the details, but things got kind of crazy. Samuel found himself — naked and high — with a knife at his throat.

He thought he was going to die.

Perhaps it was the instinct of self-preservation that kicked in through Samuel's drug-induced brain, but he turned, ran a few steps and dived out a window. Out a fourth-floor window!

Male prostitution is incredibly dangerous. Serial killers like John Wayne Gacy and Jeffrey Dahmer frequented some of the same bars that our outreach teams go into. (Some of our guys have even claimed they "dated" Dahmer.) A hustler rarely has a family that will miss him or friends that will notice his sudden disappearance. This makes him easy prey. Added to that is the fact that the customers view them as something to be used and discarded. In a guide for police on street prostitution, the United States Department of Justice states, "prostitution clients, typically referred to as 'johns' or 'tricks,' are attracted to the illicit nature of the encounter, desire sex acts that regular partners do not provide, view sex as merely a commodity, and/or lack interest in or access to conventional relationships. Others are drawn to the fact that no commitment is required, and view these interactions as less risky than having an affair."[24]

The window screen and frame cut Samuel's side and arms. The fall onto the building's metal awning over its front entrance broke his elbow and slowed his descent. The final tumble onto the sidewalk broke his ankle.

Naked, broken, high, and bleeding, he stumbled over to Emmaus leaving a trail of blood. Deacon Alfred Coleman, our ministry director at the time, and I had been in the center cleaning up from lunch when the intercom buzzer rang and we asked who it was.

"It's Samuel, let me in, I'm hurt!"

We didn't have a video camera out front to know who was at the door, so we buzzed Samuel in not knowing what to expect. He came in flailing and stumbling, his panic and intoxication evident. He staggered through our living room and into the kitchen ranting about some guy who was trying to kill him.

He could hardly walk, was bleeding badly, and his arm was twisted at a grotesque angle. Alfred dialed 911 as I corralled Samuel into one of our bathrooms and then into the shower, needing to contain him so he didn't hurt himself further. I was concerned about his blood dripping everywhere. We calmed him down, stopped the bleeding, and got some clothes on him just as the police and paramedics arrived.

You would think an experience like that would wake someone up, wouldn't you?

But no, that was just the pilot episode of a long and tragic series. The hold that the streets have on our guys is incredibly strong. Breaking free takes a relentless effort on our part to reach out to guys like Samuel and walk with them through the nightmare of their life. It also takes a realization on their part that they've hit bottom. Unfortunately, Samuel still had farther to fall. After he got out of the hospital, he tried a drug treatment program but didn't stay more than a few weeks. His drug habit had grown so bad that selling his body wasn't enough to keep up. He started ripping people off by snatching purses or backpacks and stealing from stores. He got arrested for drug possession and petty theft and ended up in jail.

We stayed in touch with him in prison, and after he was paroled we helped him secure housing at a local mission. He stayed a month and then returned to the streets. One of our outreach teams saw him hustling, but he tried to hide from them.

For a guy like Samuel, Emmaus becomes a surrogate family. When a guy whom we've helped relapses back into the streets, he often feels ashamed and tries to hide his hustling from us. But with at least one outreach team out most every night, that's hard to do. It's also hard, though, to ride this emotional roller coaster with the guys as you see them doing well and then falling back, time and time again. It's in those times, when I want to give up on a guy or just quit, that I need to let God pull me with Him or drag me along as need be. It's also in those times of difficulty that I rely on my co-workers to pray with me, support me, and encourage me.

Samuel later came by the ministry center, but got into a fight with another guy and was "barred" for three months. Although two hundred street guys visit our center each year, we rarely see acts of violence committed here. They know we demand they respect our place and the people there, or else they'll get barred. More importantly, for many of our men, Emmaus is the one safe place they know they can go to, and because of that, they try to respect our rules.

The cycle continued with Samuel for several years. We would see him on the streets using drugs, drinking, and hustling. Eventually, he would come to the center. Then we'd get him into treatment or into a shelter, but he would never stay long. He was in and out of jail. In the summer of 2004, he came by the center after three days of using crack cocaine. He could barely breathe, was staggering, and had severe chest pains. A heart attack was imminent. We called 911 and the medics took him to our local hospital. He was diagnosed with pneumonia and a heart infection.

Crack is the drug of choice for many of the guys hustling on the Chicago streets. The pervasiveness of this lethal type of cocaine has transformed low-income urban communities, especially the lives of men and women in street prostitution. Prior to the rise of cocaine in the 1980s, prostituting men and women were more likely to "to set aside money for living expenses, nice clothes, and personal hygiene, whereas now almost all of a habitual cocaine user's money is spent on the drug."[25]

Two of our staff visited Samuel in the hospital and offered him a copy of *The Life Recovery Bible*, an edition of the Bible that Tyndale House Publishers graciously gives us free. It integrates the philosophy and principles of the Twelve Steps of Alcoholics Anonymous throughout the Scriptures. It's a great tool for guys like Samuel — if you can get them to read it.

With the toll his lifestyle had taken, Samuel wasn't going anywhere and so he accepted the "Recovery Bible" and started reading. Our staff visited him throughout his hospital stay. He started talking about his family and his past. An alienated sister whom he had lied to, threatened, and robbed was contacted by our staff and came to visit. Samuel seemed genuinely broken and repentant.

A month after his near-heart attack, Samuel was moved to a nursing home. Then he stayed with his sister for several months and we had hopes that he was finally moving away from the streets, restoring his relationships with his family, and heading on to a better life. But at a staff meeting, one of our outreach members said he had seen Samuel on the streets the night before, high and hustling. Our collective heart broke. But as a former mafia "leg-breaker," recovering alcoholic, turned Catholic lay minister once told me, "Broken knuckles are like broken hearts, the more they break the bigger they get."

Samuel's relapse to the streets was brief. He got clean, did another time in treatment, and found a small studio apartment. During this time, he met two of our volunteers. Both came from a street background and could personally relate to Samuel's addiction struggles. He spent long hours in our center talking and praying with them.

Several weeks went by without Samuel falling back. Then several months. And now over six years, the longest we have known for him to be off the streets and doing well.

"I just wanted to come over and tell you guys how much I appreciate all you've done for me," he said as he stood by our car on that evening Carolyn and I were heading out for a date night. "Things are going so well for me right now. I'm working side jobs, making my recovery meetings, and praying a lot. All you guys at Emmaus have been great to me. I just want to say thanks."

Once again, I looked past him at the awning that had broken his fall. I thought about the road he's walked, the drugs he's abused, and the tricks he's turned. But Samuel isn't looking back. He's looking ahead.

The words of the parables in Luke illustrate the tender, relentless activity of a God who is seeking out and saving lost guys like Samuel. When I feel discouraged and lost myself, I grab onto God's coattails and let Him drag me along until I'm able to stand on my own once more. It's about trust and hope, all the way to the end. Even if Samuel had died on the streets, I would have trusted and hoped that something we did or said had got through to him and he had made his peace with God.

It can be tempting to think of hard-core street people as "hopeless"

or "lifers." It can get discouraging knowing so many lost and desperate people. It can make a person want to give up. That's when we need to trust and let God hold us, pull us, and, if necessary, drag us along.

I feel immensely privileged to have left some scuff marks on the sidewalk.

Listen and Reflect

Carolyn wrote "Here I Go Again" in response to hearing about Samuel's fall from the fourth floor of the building next door. Listen to this song at www.greenchoby.com/music-42.html and see how it reflects on your life.

Read and Reflect

The Book of James is perhaps the richest section of Scripture in terms of God's activity in seeking out and saving that which is lost, as well our need to partner with Him. One out of every five verses in this book speaks about God's concern for the poor.

> What good is it, my brothers and sisters, if you say you have faith but do not have works? Can faith save you? If a brother or sister is naked and lacks daily food, and one of you says to them, "Go in peace; keep warm and eat your fill," and yet you do not supply their bodily needs, what is the good of that? . . . For just as the body without the spirit is dead, so faith without works is also dead.
> — James 2:14-16,26

For Discussion

These parables from Luke can easily apply to guys on the streets lost to addiction and prostitution. But we are all lost sheep, coins, and sons.

1. How did God actively reach out to you during a time when you were lost?

2. How often do the "verses" of your life speak of God's concern for the poor and the oppressed?

3. What metaphor (such as " Footprints in the Sand" or "Scuff Marks on the Sidewalk") describes your spiritual journey?

Pray

"Pursuer of our souls, may we not go too far astray, nor hide from the light of Your lamp, or stay lost in the distant country. Run to us, Father, and call us home."

Chapter 17

God's Street-Level Deacons

When we "walk humbly with God," it's tempting to think He's taking our path. But God's ways are not our ways.

I'm an ordained permanent deacon in the Roman Catholic Church. I clocked over one thousand hours and four years of study to get to that ordination. To make me a deacon in the Church, Cardinal Francis George, Archbishop of Chicago and former president of the United States Conference of Catholic Bishops, laid hands on me in a moving ceremony in May 2002 at Holy Name Cathedral in downtown Chicago. That plus my B.A. in Christian Education and my M.A. in Educational Ministries from Wheaton College are my "credentials" for ministry. I like to think I've used those "creds" well.

The problem with credentials and degrees, though, is it's too easy to think that those of us with them are the ones who can minister and those without can't. Some people call this syndrome the "diploma disease."

Time and again, I've been humbled at how God uses what I call "street-level deacons." Jesus said that the "last shall be first." Folks whom society disregards often become the vessels of His grace. We who possess all the "creds" in the world can only hope and dream of being instruments at this level.

My first brush with God's crafty and class-less Spirit came during an impromptu early morning prayer meeting.

* * * *

I was walking down Clark Street around 2 a.m. toward a bar that's one of our outreach spots. I never made it there. About a block away, a group of guys were hanging out. One of them yelled over to me, "Yo, it's Brother John!" (as I was known on the streets at the time). I looked at these guys and saw a group from which most visitors to Chicago would steer clear. Three were clearly drunk. One was a gang enforcer complete with a beefy build and tattoos. Glazed eyes, slurred speech, and nervousness — not to mention the quart-sized bottles of Old Style that two of them carried — told me they'd all been drinking. A couple of guys I knew to be hustlers were hanging out also, plus a few more whom I didn't recognize.

I walked up to the group and shook a couple of hands. "Who the *&%# are you?" one of the guys I didn't know said as he got in my face. Before I could respond, Willie came to my defense. "Ease up, man, this is Brother John with Emmaus. He's a minister and he's cool." A look of respect came over my accuser's face and he backed off.

Then the strangest, most unexpected, glorious, thing happened. Willie, who's the local finger-breaker and enforcer for the Gangster Disciples in the area, gathered us all together and said, "Brother John, we gots ta pray!" A chorus of "Yeah, let's pray!"' followed and everybody joined in, all seven of us. The two with bottles put them down and the two guys hustling the passing cars turned from the "johns" to join us. A couple of guys who were selling fake jewelry to tourists put their chains in their pockets, and we prayed.

I felt a little silly.

Here we were, standing on this street corner, holding hands in a big circle and bowing our heads. I realized they were all waiting for me to start. Then I said a simple prayer. I didn't know quite what to do and my words were bland and churchy. I was nearing the end, and we all had our heads bowed and eyes closed, when a bright light erupted in our midst. Was an angel making its presence known or was it some other heavenly movement of God's hand?

No. I looked up, right into the spotlight of a passing Chicago Police Department cruiser. I gave the officer a sheepish smile and went back to praying. The cop probably shook his head and just kept going. I ended my prayer and started letting go of my neighbors' hands, thinking our little prayer meeting should break up before the police come back.

But nobody would let go. Willie was on my left and he began his own prayer: "JESUS! JESUS!" Some soft "amens" rippled around our circle. "OH! Jesus. JESUS, I'M HIGH! But I need you tonight, I need your forgiveness, take me away from these drugs and this drinkin', Lord."

The "amens" were much louder now as Willie launched into full-on, Pentecostal prayer mode. "Jesus, we believe!"

"Amen!"

"Jesus we need you!"

"Amen!"

"Jesus forgive us!"

The "amen" after that was one of the most heartfelt and sincere I've ever heard.

After Willie finished, each guy prayed something. When the prayer circle came back to me, I led the group in the Our Father and all God's people said, "Amen!"

It was an amazing night. I walked away from that group marveling at how God was at work on the streets.

Several years later, I marveled once again at how God used a crack-addicted, prostituting man as His "street-level deacon" to help us get a twelve-year-old boy off the streets.

* * * *

The kid and the seagull seemed to be playing tag. In the early morning the area surrounding the soccer field in the park near our house is covered with gulls and pigeons. It was about eight o'clock and the sun was mostly up over Lake Michigan. The birds were feeding off the trash left by the crowds that had cheered the soccer matches on nearby fields the night before.

My then eight-month-old son Jonathan and I were there because about three or four times a week we walked a three-mile route along the lakefront early in the morning. He actually just rode in the backpack carrier that his mule, I mean father, got to carry.

Ahead of us, a lone seagull flew away from its many friends and a young boy chased it. The bird flew low along the ground for several feet and landed. The boy chased it until it took off again.

Baggy blue jeans and a flannel shirt were all the child wore to ward off the cold of this early September morning. Approaching, I saw his dark hair, round face, and Eastern European features. Standing in the trees off to the side, I noticed a woman and a man stuffing blankets into their bags, having probably just awoken in the park. The kid seemed to be with them. It made me sad to see a homeless family waking up, outside, on such a cold morning. It was a picture of a family trying to make the best of what they have. Jonathan and I waved hello and I said, "Good morning." They nodded greetings in return, and Jonathan and I kept walking toward home.

Several days later Carolyn was out walking our dog and pushing Jonathan in the stroller when a crack-addicted hustler name Jerry stopped her. "You gotta talk with that kid!" he blurted, and she had no idea what he was talking about. "There he go," Jerry continued and pointed. "That's the one. His name's Christopher. Carolyn, he ain't nothing but twelve years old and he's out hustling those cars!" She watched as Christopher rode a beat-up bike into the parking lot near the park.

The lot's about a half mile from our home, and almost any time, day or night, you'll see cars slowly driving around. These are nice cars — SUVs and sedans — and the drivers appear well off. These men are looking for anonymous, usually one-time sexual encounters with other men. Sometimes they pick up one of the prostituting men that circle the parking lot looking for a trick. It's called "cruising," and it happens all over the place, in large city parks like this one and in smaller rural and suburban areas as well. The anonymity and easy access to the park make it desirable for those looking to solicit a prostitute.

As Michael Scott and Kelly Dedel point out, "Clients' decision to solicit a prostitute is influenced by availability of prostitutes, knowledge of where to find them, access to money, perceived risk of getting caught or contracting disease, and ease of securing services."[26]

Jerry was livid. His concern for Christopher seemed real and urgent. Fortunately, it didn't take much to get Jerry talking, so he gabbed while he and Carolyn watched Christopher riding around the parking lot. As she listened, Carolyn tried to discern whether Jerry was high and if his story was believable.

"I made my mistakes," he said. "I know that. But that BOY don't have no business down here! I saw him getting out of a car the other day and I asked him what was he doin'. He just waved one hundred dollars in my face and said, 'Making my money.' He walked right over to his mom and handed her some of the money. All she does is go to the liquor store and buy herself some drink. She's just using that boy, just like all these old men out here are."

Jerry's words and concern coupled with the evidence before Carolyn's eyes launched her into action. Before Jonathan's birth, Carolyn was a caseworker at Central Baptist Family Services for several years. She's all too familiar with broken families and the horrific burdens young children often bear.

That morning, Carolyn left Jerry and approached Christopher while she pushed the stroller, our mutt Mandy panting at her side. Her motherly appearance probably enabled her to gain an ounce of trust from Christopher. She inquired about his parents and what he was doing, but the young boy wouldn't reply. His blue eyes never met Carolyn's as he watched the passing cars, but he patted Mandy on the head.

When Carolyn returned home, she called the police and the Department of Children and Family Services (DCFS). Later that day, an officer called and informed her they were holding Christopher at the local hospital where he went for help with a cut on his arm. Carolyn went down and told the officer what she knew but made sure that Christopher didn't see her. He denied hustling and living in the park and told the officer that he lived with his grandmother on Sheridan Road. The officer drove him to his grandmother's, but the next day Christopher was back hustling in the parking lot.

Carolyn's protective and maternal instinct kicked into full swing. A few days later, she packed a PB&J sandwich and headed to the skate park, hoping to run into Christopher. She found him and he accepted the sandwich, munching it while Carolyn attempted shallow conversation. She got few answers. She encouraged him to come by Emmaus before leaving. When she returned home, both of us were convinced we should adopt Christopher to save him from the streets.

Thanks to Carolyn's persistent investigating, within a few weeks we learned more about the young boy. He had been taken away from his mother once before but had run away from a foster-family placement. "He's not gonna change," a social worker told Carolyn over the phone. We learned that Christopher's older sister had prostituted also. We also found out that since Christopher's mother was homeless, it was hard for DCFS to track her down to issue a complaint or to start an investigation.

Then several of our guys noticed Christopher hustling at another spot. They tried to talk him into coming by Emmaus, but he wouldn't trust an organization — he thought we'd simply call the police.

During all this, our family was working a weekly soup kitchen at our Catholic parish. With Jonathan riding in a backpack carrier, I walked among the tables of homeless people ladling out soup. I stopped short at one table when I recognized Christopher, his mom, and a guy who seemed to be her (or his) pimp. I wanted to dump the soup on the two adults' heads and snatch Christopher out of there!

It was several more weeks of frustrating back and forth with the police and DCFS before we got a call that Christopher was in protective custody. He had gone to the hospital with a broken arm. Perhaps it was a mishap on the playground, but more likely it was caused by his mom's "boyfriend" or an angry trick. The injury got the police involved again and DCFS picked him up.

We tried to find out what had happened to Christopher, but the state officials we spoke with wouldn't release any information.

He's often in my prayers.

* * * *

There are a lot of "Christophers" out there. Statistics from the United States Department of Justice estimate that up to three million children under the age of eighteen are involved in prostitution in our country.[27]

Without Jerry, one of God's "street-level deacons," this young boy might have died at the hands of some "trick," from an overdose, or because of the violence that rocks the streets. God used Jerry to bring change to a young boy's harsh life.

A year or so after Christopher was removed from the streets, Jerry's body was found in an alley about two miles from our house. He had been murdered. No one was ever caught or convicted of the crime. With no degrees or diplomas to his name, Jerry was nevertheless an instrument of God's grace and mercy in a young boy's life. Truly an amazing grace.

Digging Deeper

Listen and Reflect

Carolyn wrote "Christopher's Song" while we were working with the police and family services to get him into a group home. Listen to it at www.greenchoby.com/music-18.html.

Read and Reflect

Do not look forward to the changes and the chances of this life in fear; rather look to them with full hope that, as they arise, God, whose you are, will deliver you out of them. He is your keeper. He has kept you hitherto. Do but hold fast to his dear hand, and he will lead you safely through all things; and, when you cannot stand, he will bear you in his arms. Do not look forward to what may happen tomorrow. Our Father will either shield you from suffering, or he will give you strength to bear it.

— St. Francis de Sales

For Discussion

1. How often do you seek to control the path God has for you?

2. How is losing that control a part of the spiritual life?

3. Have you ever been surprised by God working through unlikely "deacons" in your own life?

Pray

"For all who are lost and forsaken, send to them, Father, Your unlikely saints and deacons to show them the path of life."

Chapter 18

God in a World of Hurt

I've often wondered how the Good Samaritan (Lk 10:25-37) would have responded if the road between Jerusalem and Jericho had been littered with people in need? Would he have helped the one stranger but not the others? Would he have taken a different path?

When my thoughts drift this way, I'm reminded of a story of Blessed Teresa of Calcutta visiting Manhattan. Her guide was British author Malcolm Muggeridge. One day they had a few hours to kill before their next engagement, which was only about eight blocks away. Since it was a beautiful spring day, Mother asked if they could walk. Muggeridge saw no problem with this, and they started their stroll down the sidewalk. But after almost three hours and with the time of their appointment nearing, they were still two blocks from their destination. Muggeridge finally hailed a cab so they could arrive on time.

It wasn't that Mother Teresa was a slow walker but every time she encountered a homeless person or someone begging, she stopped to see how she could help. While bending over and talking with a man lying on the sidewalk, she sent one of her Sisters into a local store to beg for a blanket to cover him. When a woman asked her for food, she herself went into a restaurant and begged for a meal. With others, she simply sat, talking and praying with them. She did what she could to help any person in need, and that was why it took her so long to cover so short a distance.

I wish I were more like Mother Teresa. I've walked by hundreds of homeless people. I've helped quite a few, but I've only tossed a glance at many others. How do I reconcile this? How do I walk through a world of hurt and broken people and not get overwhelmed? I wish I could always live with the same spirit of Mother Teresa. I wish we all could. But until we get to that place, we have to make do with current realities.

The Parable of the Good Samaritan and this story of Mother Teresa remind me of the importance of one life. I may not be able to help every hurting, broken, homeless, and poor person with whom my life intersects, but I can help one person at a time. And I can trust that his or her humble path with God and my humble path with God — scuff marks and all — have crossed for a reason.

You never know what will transpire from these humble intersections. You have to trust that God is in control. He puts people in our path to give us the opportunity to help them, but often He puts people in our path to teach us, mold us, to shape us . . . to make us holy. Steve was one of those guys God put in my path whom I thought I was there to help. But it wasn't Steve's life that changed me; it was his death.

* * * *

Steve sat at the edge of death as I sat in a plastic chair next to his hospital bed. Looking at him, all I could think about was the movie *Dead Man Walking*.

In that film, Sister Helen Prejean — with passion, hope, and desperation mixing equally in her voice — tells convicted murderer and rapist Matthew Poncelet, "Look at me! I want the last face you see in this world to be a face of love!"

A face of love.

At Emmaus, that's what we try so hard to be every day: God's face of love to guys who have rarely received even a glance of compassion, concern, or caring directed their way. Through outreach and counseling, through home-cooked meals at our table in the ministry center, through facilities where they can get a shower and do their laundry, through sitting by their bedside when they're in the hospital, we show these men a face of love.

And Steve, dying of AIDS at thirty-seven, needed to see a face of love right then.

He had floated in and out of consciousness for a while and, considering his condition, it was surprising that he hadn't already died. Tuberculosis, bronchitis, and pneumonia were waging an interior battle to stop his breathing and collapse his lungs. A blood infection caused his blood pressure to drop at times. His kidneys had failed, but dialysis seemed to be helping. Because of a skin infection, bluish-red and purple lesions blanketed most of his lower body. And he probably had prostate cancer.

Life wasn't always like this for Steve.

He had grown up outside of Memphis and with his soft drawl, easy smile, and friendly spirit, you'd never guess that this pale, lanky Tennessean carried a deep well of pain that stemmed from his having a physically abusive and sadistic father.

One time he told me he had a baby rabbit when he was little. When it got loose from its cage and chewed at the base of some furniture, his father killed the bunny and put its body on the front steps for Steve to find coming home from school. All he remembers is standing on the steps looking at his little pet while his father towered over him and screamed, "I told you! I told you to take care of that rabbit!"

The physical beatings Steve endured were random and violent. Often his father was arrested when a teacher or neighbor saw the bruises and called the police — but he was never gone long enough. As soon as Steve could, he fled that home and ended up on the streets looking for a way to survive. Homelessness and poverty led him to prostitution as a means of survival.

Steve embodied the question, "How could this happen to such a nice person?" He was a joy to be around. He made friends quicker than most. He brightened a room by just walking into it. He was lovable, kind, and generous. He even had Winnie the Pooh tattooed on his belly — Winnie the Pooh!

I often have Steve in mind when I speak about our work and tell people, "These are nice guys!" Men who have resorted to prostitution as a way to survive see what they do as harmless. They don't want to steal cars, gangbang, or rob people, so prostitution seems like a way to make money without causing harm.

They really are nice guys!

It's hard to point to the one thing that put Steve in the hospital. He had stopped prostituting and using crack a year earlier, had managed to get himself on Social Security Disability and used that money to rent an apartment next door to Emmaus. But that past winter, whenever he dropped by Emmaus to visit, he looked more and more depressed. His usual easygoing manner was absent. Then in January, he phoned Sill, our ministry director.

"I just called to say goodbye," he rasped. He spoke between deep breaths that seemed to take more effort than he had. "I stopped eating about two weeks ago, Sill. I just want to die." *Click*.

Sill and a volunteer rushed to Steve's apartment and found him emaciated and semi-conscious. Sill dialed 911. The ambulance carried Steve a few blocks to Weiss Hospital where he had remained. A month into his stay, he had to be put on a respirator. The hospital chaplain called Emmaus and asked for Katie Yee, our assistant ministry director. Steve had listed her as his emergency contact, and the chaplain wanted her to know Steve had been put on a respirator.

These kinds of relationships — this kind of guy — are why Emmaus exists. The former prostitute who doesn't know where else to turn when he tries to leave the street. The guy who lists us as an emergency contact because he trusts that we'll be there, that we care.

And so we visited Steve. Almost every day somebody from Emmaus walked the few blocks to Weiss to spend time sitting beside his bed: reading him some Scripture, telling him a story, or simply being present in silence. Carolyn came to the hospital one day, and a nurse pulled her aside. "Who is this guy?" the nurse asked her while pointing her thumb at Steve's sleeping form behind the thin privacy curtain in the room he shared with four others. "There's all these people coming up to visit him, and the cards, flowers and whatnot. . . . Who is this guy?"

The nurse was perplexed because she knew Steve was on one of the indigent floors the hospital had for street people who live in our community. Those patients usually don't get many visitors. Carolyn simply said, "He's a friend, and he's precious to God," and drew back the curtain to, once again, show Steve a face of love.

Every month on a Saturday afternoon, Paul Horcher battles traffic into Chicago to share a family-style meal at the Emmaus Ministry Center and hang out with our guys. This forty-six-year-old father of six responded to God's nudges to volunteer at Emmaus, but as a former dairy farmer and the owner of a suburban construction company, Paul finds city life foreign. Steve was one of the first guys he met. "He always came up to me with that warm smile and big laugh," Paul said. "I felt welcome in his world."

After Paul learned Steve had been hospitalized and wasn't expected to live, he visited Steve and later wrote this reflection:

> At the hospital, I struggled with going in the room. Would he recognize me? I was just another volunteer from Emmaus — not a great friend who really knew him. Heck, I didn't even know his last name. But I finally went in. His face was very thin and gaunt. His arms and legs were extremely swollen. He had painful looking discolored marks on the rest of his body. He was clearly in pain. He had a confused look in his eyes.
>
> "'Hello, Steve. I am Paul from Emmaus. Do you remember me?" The confusion went away. He blinked as if to say, "Yes, I know you." He couldn't speak. I didn't want to touch his hands because they looked so painful, so I put my hand on his head. I didn't know what to say other than, "God loves you, Steve" and "You are God's beloved child — especially now." He blinked again, then grimaced in severe pain several times, and the nurse came in to tend to him.
>
> In the waiting room, I prayed the Rosary for Steve and for guidance. When I went back in, I said the few words that formed in my mouth and left shortly after, feeling completely unsettled. The next day in prayer, I reflected on my time with Steve — why I felt so thrown off balance by it.

Then it hit me — it was Jesus Christ in that bed. He was suffering with and for Steve. It was His face that was so gaunt, His hands and feet that were so swollen, His body that was scarred and discolored, and His eyes that blinked at me. But He was also in the loud laughter that rolled so easily from Steve's mouth, and He was in the warmth and joy that Steve's presence brought into a room. Emmaus has helped me to discover that in our brokenness we meet Christ. In our joy we meet Christ. In sharing myself with the guys at Emmaus, I meet Christ.

Steve died on May 25, 2007. We held a memorial for him at a local church. People from all walks of life came. Staff and volunteers from Emmaus and several other ministries were on hand. Homeless people and men and women in prostitution filled the pews. I gave a short sermon and then we opened the microphone for people to share. The testimonies were heartfelt and touched me deeply. Even in the midst of his addiction and pain, Steve had an amazing impact on so many people.

Many pieces of the puzzle that was Steve fell into place during those testimonies. Lisa Martin, a former Emmaus staff member came to the microphone and shared how, when Steve was sedated and on the respirator, she sat in the chair next to him and prayed for healing. But through the Holy Spirit's prompting, she found herself praying for Steve to recover long enough to be reconciled to his family and to God.

Next, Sill told how Steve, in a rare moment of lucidity, had whispered a simple request to him: "Find my family." Sill had tried to contact Steve's family in Memphis with little success. Little did he know that their phone bill had gone unpaid for several months and their service had been cut off.

Toward the end of Steve's life, Sill tried the number once more. The call went through and Steve's sister answered. Her phone bill was still unpaid and the service remained disconnected, but somehow Sill's call rang through. It was the only call she had received in months! After hearing that her brother was dying, she and another sister traveled to Chicago and stayed with Steve long enough to forgive him and be forgiven by him. They sat by his side to the end, showing him the face of love.

The next speaker at the memorial service was a staff member from another nearby ministry who shared how hard it was for Steve to talk about his faith in God. Several years ago, Steve had said to her, "I love God, but I don't think God could love me." Then, a few short weeks before his death, as she visited Steve at his bedside, he turned, looked into her face of love and simply said, "I know now that God loves me."

There was a quiet, prayerful silence in the church. The presence of God was tangible and comforting. It touched all of us.

And then the police arrived.

Well, at least one of them. As I was closing the service and preparing for a final prayer, an African-American, Chicago police officer in full uniform strode up the center aisle. Her bulletproof vest and black utility belt with gun and handcuffs made her seem larger than her petite frame. She walked right up to me and asked if she could say a few words.

One of my cardinal rules for leading a memorial service is that if someone with a gun, Taser, handcuffs, and industrial-strength pepper spray asks to say a few words, you don't argue with her. So I stepped aside.

"I was across the street just now when someone gave me a flier about this service," she began. "When I saw who it was for, I just knew I had to come over. I've known Steve for several years. The first time I met him I was arresting him for disorderly conduct. As he sat in my squad car, handcuffed in the back seat, he just turned that smile of his on me and said, 'Honey, you are too gorgeous to be a cop!' That made me laugh!

"That was the start of a strange but beautiful friendship. Whenever I saw him on the street, he'd come over to my car and say hello. When he found out I was a singer, he'd not only come over but he'd get in the back of my car and demand I sing for him. We spent quite a few times in that car singing Gospel tunes. So, Steve, this one's for you."

The officer stepped back from the mic and a deep, rich, beautiful and haunting rendition of "His Eye Is on the Sparrow" echoed through the church. I doubt there was a dry eye in the whole church by the time she sang the closing refrain:

> I sing because I'm happy,
> I sing because I'm free,
> For His eye is on the sparrow,
> And I know He watches me.

* * * *

When I first met Steve I thought I was the one who was there to help him. But all the help I could offer didn't keep him from dying.

Steve's humble path with God crossed so many others during his time on this earth. Many of us thought God had brought us together to make a difference in this poor, crack-addicted, prostituting man's life. But in meeting him and journeying with him we were the changed ones.

The streets are littered with lives like Steve's. For a Good Samaritan walking those streets it can seem overwhelming. I know I can't help all the "Steves" I come across. But, by God, I can help one at a time. And if — like Mother Teresa's covering a few blocks in Manhattan — that means my walk is delayed, so be it. It's a small price to pay for showing a face of love.

Digging Deeper

Listen and Reflect

Carolyn's song "Little Mo' Wisdom" can be listened to at www. greenchoby.com/music-46.html. We can all use a little more wisdom and humility when it comes to our walk with God.

Read and Reflect

Antoine de Saint-Exupéry, the French author of *The Little Prince*, once wrote, "If you want to build a ship, don't drum up the men to gather wood, divide the work, and give orders. Instead, teach them to yearn for the vast and endless immensity of the sea."[28]

For Discussion

1. How does the quote from Saint-Exupéry relate to the story of Steve?

2. What would you have done if you were walking those few blocks in New York City with Mother Teresa?

3. What is most scandalous to you in the story of Steve's life and death?

4. What is most inspiring?

Pray

"God our Father, as our humble journeys cross paths with Your poor, help us to respond with love and compassion and not glance away."

Chapter 19

A God Who Listens

"Hear my prayer, O Lord; give ear to my supplications in your faithfulness; answer me in your righteousness." So begins Psalm 143. David seemed to be in some type of trouble when he penned this plea. Perhaps his son Absalom was trying to kill him. Whatever the circumstances, he clearly struggled with desolation and anguish. He desperately needed to hear from God.

By now, you know I don't believe in doing ministry for the "warm fuzzies." I do what I do because this is the mission to which God has called me. At times I get discouraged and depressed and I begin the slide into a pool of desolation. When this happens, I have to remind myself that walking humbly with God isn't walking by myself. God isn't a silent companion on my journey. He's ready and willing to listen to prayer and also equally willing to give an answer.

When I'm down, when it feels like I'm living a present-day Psalm 143, I tell God to give me an answer. That may seem a bit arrogant, but I've learned not to mince words with the Almighty. My prayer in those times seems almost feral and savage. No flowery words, no striving for the poetic imagery that might impress the Creator of the Universe. I simply beg God to give me some hint that my labor is not in vain.

Sometimes I've been extremely specific in my prayer. When I was looking for a new spiritual director, I asked God to help me find a retired Catholic priest who had been a missionary in Japan, lived a deeply spiritual life and had a very cool contemplative Japanese garden in his backyard, complete with neatly raked stone field and koi pond. The Lord ended up leading me to Martha, a Catholic laywoman, poet and retired farmer who lives on a thirty-acre wooded retreat center with her husband, David. I cut the Lord some slack; it wasn't exactly what I had asked for but came pretty close.

A few years ago, I was in my office and felt myself beginning to slide. We had recently buried three guys who had been killed by the many dangers inherent with living on the street. Their deaths were weighing on me. Donations were down and I didn't know if we'd make it through the upcoming summer. One of our "success stories" had arrived the day before, drunk and belligerent, and we had to call the police to have him removed from the ministry center.

As I sat at my computer trying to write the next month's newsletter nothing was working. I'd start typing a few lines and then find my right pinkie pressing the backspace key — all the words I had written disappeared, swept away by the cursor. I started musing that this was like our ministry with the guys: get a few sentences of a healthy life on their page and then watch it get wiped out. Written, deleted, written, deleted. It was all a sad joke.

My hands came off the keyboard and my palms pressed into my eye sockets as I cradled my face in despair. The savage prayers followed. I'm not sure what I said or thought, but it wasn't pretty. I simply ended my prayer asking God for a boost, something far beyond my often afternoon pick-me-up — a Starbucks Venti Java Chip Frappicino with an extra shot of espresso.

Then Larry knocked on my door.

I met Larry when he was first getting clean and sober in the very early years of our ministry, around 1992. Formerly homeless and a recovering addict, he is extremely gifted in reaching guys on the street. We stayed in touch, and in 2001 he joined the Emmaus staff. His dreadlocks and beard are graying a bit on the edges now, betraying his age of forty-nine. His has not been an easy life, but his example of a godly man who's overcome many of the same challenges our guys have faced has blessed our ministry immensely. Today he is on staff with the Navigators ministry in Chicago, concentrating on engaging college and university students in urban ministry.

But this day, Larry was knocking at my door to tell me about the night before.

* * * *

Larry had been doing outreach on a Monday night a couple weeks earlier. As he was talking with two of our student volunteers from Moody Bible Institute, he noticed a young hustler approaching him.

This particular spring we became aware of a number of younger guys prostituting. By young, I mean fourteen- to eighteen-year-olds. This is a somewhat new phenomenon in Chicago. When I started Emmaus in 1990, I rarely ran into kids that age on the street. Now, twenty years later, we see them every week. The rise of alternative lifestyles, the continuing breakdown of our families, and the early sexualization of youth through media and peer pressure all probably contribute to this changing dynamic on the streets. This new, younger crowd is a challenge to reach. The fact that many of our volunteer outreach ministers are college students helps a lot. But many teenagers have an attitude of invulnerability, and that's no different with teens on the streets. They think they will beat the streets rather than be beaten by them. Sometimes only after many years of street life do they finally realize how wrong they were. We try to reach them before that happens.

As Larry finished giving his college volunteers pointers on street outreach, he sent them across the avenue to talk with some guys hanging out on the corner near a Starbucks. Larry then turned to Jamal who was swaggering toward him.

"Yo! What's up, Larry?" Jamal smacked Larry's hand, grabbed it, and did a quick handshaking and finger-snapping routine that I can't even begin to describe.

"You being safe tonight, Jamal?" Larry asked as the kid eyed a passing trick in a car.

"Safe? Whatchu you talkin' 'bout? You don't have to worry about me, Larry. It's these 'marks' out here that you need to worry about. Any of them try something with me, I'll bust them up." Jamal launches into a tirade about how a "mark" (customer) tried something on him, and Jamal "taught him a lesson."

Jamal told Larry he was twenty, but he looked around sixteen. He had a sparkle in his eyes that wasn't yet dulled by the streets. But an arrogance in those eyes probably blinded him from seeing the streets as they really are. Plus, he couldn't have weighed more than one hundred thirty pounds. He was slight, dark-skinned, and appeared very confident.

"I'm the king out here, Larry. I'm in control. I don't go with no one nowhere, and I don't do nothing I don't wanna. I'm making large cash out here, and I don't have to answer to nobody."

Jamal started to go on about how tough he was, but Larry had heard enough bull for one night.

"So, Jamal, what you're telling me is that you like being somebody's sex toy? You like selling yourself to these marks. And you like getting thrown away when they're done playing with you. Is that what you're telling me, is that what you like doing?"

Larry's real subtle like that.

Jamal stopped his swaggering and seemed to deflate before Larry's eyes. He looked at Larry for a while, but didn't say a word. Then he just turned around and left. Larry felt he had pushed too hard, but there was no taking back his words.

A week went by. Larry and his faithful volunteers were back out the following Monday night, when he saw a large car driving slowly around the block. On its second pass, he spotted Jamal sitting in the passenger's seat and a large African-American man driving. Jamal pointed to Larry and the car pulled over. When they both got out and started walking toward him, Larry didn't know what to expect.

"There he is, that's the one," Larry overheard Jamal say to the driver as they got closer.

Larry watched as the two approached. The man towered over the slight Jamal. He was dressed casually and walked with confidence. Larry stood his ground and when they reached him, Jamal didn't say a word.

"Hello," the driver said in a deep, baritone voice. "My name's Sam. I wanted to thank you for sending my son home."

Before Larry knew what was happening, Sam was shaking his hand.

"Jamal ran away several weeks ago," the dad continued. "He's been using drugs, wouldn't stop, so I kicked him out. My wife and I have been worried sick. He came home last week and said a street minister had helped him wake up, see what he was doing and come to his senses. Thank you. Thank you for talking some sense into my son."

They talked for a while longer, then the pair turned and headed back to their car. As they got in and drove away, Jamal smiled and waved. His eyes still sparkled, not in arrogance, but with that glint of a prodigal son who's woken up and come to his senses.

After Larry left my office I quietly apologized to God for my lack of faith.

****

As I think back, I've probably been at that point of despair a half dozen times. Each time I've started the slide, I've prayed those savage prayers and God has listened. Larry's recount of Jamal was by far the quickest and most direct response! Usually my prayers are answered in more subtle ways: a letter from a guy whom I hadn't seen in years describing how well he was doing, a call from a participant in our immersion nights saying what a life-changing experience it had been, or a visit with a guy in the ministry center who encouraged me and gave me hope.

God's answers are many and varied, and they don't always take the same shape and size. But there is always an answer.

Digging Deeper

Listen and Reflect

"Opened Up," which can be found at www.greenchoby.com/music-10. html, describes the process of opening up to a closer and deeper walk with God on the journey of life.

Read and Reflect

"In the same way, you who are younger must accept the authority of the elders. And all of you must clothe yourselves with humility in your dealings with one another, for 'God opposes the proud, but gives grace to the humble.' Humble yourselves therefore under the mighty hand of God, so that he may exalt you in due time" (1 Pt 5:5-6).

For Discussion

1. What makes it difficult to wait upon God's "due time"?

2. What disciplines/practices do you use to keep that connection with the Lord strong?

3. How can prayer be savage?

4. When have you received a direct answer to one of your prayers?

Pray

"Lord of all grace and mercy, forgive our times of despair and help us to cling to You in our need."

Chapter 20

What Does the Lord Require of Me?

For several months, Carolyn and I have been leading a discussion group on Wednesday mornings in our soft-lit basement chapel. A life-size reprint of Rembrandt's *Return of the Prodigal Son* hangs in the front, offering a powerful visual reminder of the Father's tender, unrelenting love. Guys drop by our ministry center about an hour before lunch, and we sit on chairs in a circle and reflect on a passage from the Gospels. We are introducing them to the ancient practice called *Lectio Divina*. It is a quiet, reflective way to read Scripture and open yourself to hearing the Holy Spirit. This practice is familiar to most monks, but not to many prostituting men.

One day we read John 15:1-8:

> "I am the true vine, and my Father is the vinegrower. He
> removes every branch in me that bears no fruit. Every
> branch that bears fruit he prunes to make it bear more
> fruit. You have already been cleansed by the word that
> I have spoken to you. Abide in me as I abide in you. Just
> as the branch cannot bear fruit by itself unless it abides
> in the vine, neither can you unless you abide in me. I
> am the vine, you are the branches. Those who abide
> in me and I in them bear much fruit, because apart
> from me you can do nothing. Whoever does not abide
> in me is thrown away like a branch and withers; such
> branches are gathered, thrown into the fire, and burned.
> If you abide in me, and my words abide in you, ask for
> whatever you wish, and it will be done for you. My Father
> is glorified by this, that you bear much fruit and become
> my disciples."

Then we asked the guys to share a word or a phrase that stood out to
them, and perhaps what God was trying to tell them through it. The room
got very quiet.

After a few more silent moments, Samuel — who, as you may recall
from Chapter Sixteen, once jumped from a fourth-floor window — spoke
up but kept his eyes down, focused on the carpet. He quietly said, "It
sounds like God is begging." The silence resumed and Samuel continued
to stare at the carpet. Many years have passed since Samuel made that
dive. Some were rocky years, filled with relapses and remorse, but overall
there's been a steady progress in his new life of faith and recovery. He's
working part time now, volunteering regularly at Emmaus, leading a choir
at his church, and living right.

He continued, "It sounds like God is begging us to remain. I've never
thought of God begging me for anything. It's always me who is begging
Him. I know what I should be doing, and I know that it hurts me when I'm
not doing it. I never thought it hurt God. Maybe that's why He loves us so."

A ripple of "yeahs" and soft "amens" arose from the group. A few other
guys shared what the passage meant to them. Then the conversation
returned to Samuel.

"There's a lot of branches of the vine here at Emmaus. I've spent hours and hours talking with the staff and volunteers here. Each and every time they have built up my spirit. I know I've failed, I know I've messed up, but I know this is the place I can go to get back on the right track."

There were more "yeahs" and "amens" from the guys gathered in this quiet basement chapel. I noticed how they were looking at Samuel. In some ways, he was no longer "one of them." Several guys in the group had gotten high and prostituted the night before. Others were just a few fragile days or weeks into their journey off the street, and the grip that the darkness has on them was still evident. But they looked at Samuel with eyes of respect and perhaps even desire for what he now had. Most knew his story. They knew the work that God had done in his life had not been quick or easy. But they saw the evidence of what moving off the street meant and they wanted that for themselves.

On that morning, in that basement, he had said only a few reflective words, but it was clear that he was a branch that was bearing much fruit.

A place of many branches. Nice metaphor for Emmaus Ministries. Staff, guys, volunteers, donors, prayer partners — we all make up branches that support these guys. What we allow them to do at Emmaus is put down some roots. Life on the streets doesn't let them do that. They're always looking for the next meal, the next trick, the next high. But at Emmaus, we can provide a surrogate home, the warmth of family, self-respect, and love. Being on the streets is an exhausting way to live, so Emmaus offers guys a place to rest as they learn to live in God's restoring grace.

I think we miss Jesus' point if we look at the passage in John I just quoted as simply meeting the physical needs of the poor. The men who come by our ministry center are very hungry, but that hunger is much deeper than a lack of food in their bellies. It is a hunger for family. It is a thirst for a meaningful life. It is a desire to be welcomed into a true home, something most of them have never experienced. It is a yearning to put on the new clothes of self-respect and self-worth that the shame of prostitution has stolen from them. It is a need for people to visit them in the midst of the sickness and imprisonment of addiction and show them hope.

It is a hunger for God.

When we minister together as God's vines and branches, we can do amazing things. During the last twenty years, Emmaus Ministries has been built not by John and Carolyn Green, but by God. The Lord has called many people to make this work a reality. More than fifty people have served as staff or as interns. They, along with hundreds of volunteers and thousands of supporters have collaborated to build the branches needed to get men off the streets.

And it has been a joy to watch.

I've certainly felt God at my side, dragging me at times, but always present on this journey. But I've also known that the Body of Christ was upholding me, praying for me and our staff, sacrificially supporting our work financially, and responding to needs.

We do not walk humbly with God by ourselves. We walk in the midst of a host of witnesses who are strengthening, supporting, and guiding us on this journey.

The guys, like Samuel, whom I have witnessed make it off the streets, recognize this. The process of leaving prostitution and getting off the streets entails a stripping away of all those negative, evil voices and influences that sometimes speak in your life, too. Many of those dark powers and principalities are dug in deep in the lives of our guys. Breaking free is a long journey. Some don't make it.

But many like Samuel do. Shawn (whom I wrote about in Chapter Nine) did also, and it was a joy to watch that unfold.

* * * *

The silly grin on my face seemed misplaced in these circumstances. My six-year-old son, Daniel, sat in the church pew doubled over and vomiting on the floor. I still smiled as his upchuck splattered on to the pant legs of my tux. It wasn't the knowledge of a father of four young children who knew that this little fellow was just dehydrated and only required water and a nap to recover. I just knew that nothing was going to spoil this day.

About an hour earlier, I had stood in the front of the church next to Shawn. Ten years before this, he had come to my door, asking to be let in so he could clean up the cut on his scalp. Later, he had yelled and screamed at me as his crack addiction reared its ugly head. He had lived with Carolyn and me for a year and a half as he struggled to get a job and learn how to read. I stood next to Shawn on this bright spring day in 2010 as one of two best men in his wedding.

We looked sharp in our tuxes, so I was glad Daniel waited until after the service to get sick. But nothing was going to take my smile away. Shawn had walked a long journey. As I looked over the congregation, I saw a small glimpse of the diverse Body of Christ that had helped Shawn arrive at this day. There were staff and volunteers from Emmaus, and a supporter and his wife who had employed Shawn for several years. There was his doctor who walked with him during years of repairing the damage that almost twenty years of street life had done to his body. I saw the many faces from this small, African-American South Side church who knew Shawn as a young boy attending church with his aunt who raised him. These members prayed for him year after year during his long prodigal journey in the "distant country," and also helped disciple and nurture his faith over the last ten years.

The previous night I had hosted a party at a Chicago South Side pizza joint for the men who were important in Shawn's life. About thirty of us gathered around a large table. After devouring some deep-dish pizza, wings, and several pitchers of soda, the men had started sharing about Shawn one by one.

Sitting beside me was Anthony, a well-dressed bussinessman who knew Shawn from church. At one point, Anthony leaned toward me and said, "You know what I love about Shawn? It's that he's a soul-winner. He's always bringing folks to church, sometimes giving them a job or just helping them out for a while. He draws people to him who need God and he points them the way forward."

Later, a man from Tennessee stood up and confirmed Anthony's assessment. "My life was going downhill a couple years ago, but Shawn took me under his wing and gave me a job. He let me stay at his house and took me to church. I found God at that church because of Shawn. Even though I now live out of town, I needed to come here and say thanks." The friend walked over and gave Shawn a bear hug.

Tears welled in their eyes and mine. Few of the men gathered around this table knew Shawn's past as deeply as I did. He'd never shied away from sharing his personal history, but he didn't broadcast it either. The Tennessean saw Shawn as a successful business owner of a small landscape company, an (almost) newlywed, an upstanding and respected member of his church. I saw these things too but from a vantage point of knowing where Shawn had come from to get where he was that day.

The following afternoon Shawn, the wedding party, and I stood in front of the church and watched his fiancée, Marilyn, make her way forward in a dazzling white dress. I felt so humbled by God to be standing there and so thankful for being one small part of that cloud of witnesses that made a difference in this man's life.

A bunch of "what ifs" cascade through my mind. What if I had not closed that door on Shawn and shown him some "tough love"? What if one of our supporters hadn't hired him and taught him landscaping? What if one of our church partners hadn't bought Shawn his first truck? What if this church community hadn't welcomed back their prodigal son? How much fruit would have been lost from this broken-but-redeemed branch?

* * * *

Engaging in ministry among God's wayward sons is not for those who seek instant "warm fuzzies." But there are amazing lessons to learn while breaking bread with these prodigal sons. Lessons of justice, of mercy, of humility.

So much of our modern culture pulls us away from engagement with the poor. Perhaps God is begging us to remain.

1. How has reading this book influenced your approach to living justly?

2. In what ways have the stories in this book impacted your practice of showing mercy?

3. Has your humble walk with God been shaped or changed by this book?

Appendix I

How You Can Help

Top Ten Ways to Be Involved in the Mission of Emmaus Ministries!

1. Sign up to receive our monthly newsletter . . . and share it with your friends and family!

Each month we tell compelling stories and give people a glimpse into God's redemptive power at work in the darkest places in our culture. We offer the newsletter by e-mail and postal mail.

2. Become a "Fan" of Emmaus on Facebook.

If you're a Facebook member, join our fan base! We update this page several times a week with info about Emmaus and prayer requests for our ministry. You can find us as at www.facebook.com/emmauschicago.

3. Pray regularly for Emmaus.

Pray for our men: those who've made it off the streets, those who are struggling, and those who are still lost. Pray for our staff and volunteers, that God might protect us and use us mightily in the lives of these men. If you'd like a tool for more specific prayer, sign up to receive our monthly prayer-focused e-mail.

4. Contribute financially to Emmaus.

Financial support is critical to our work. About 1,500 individuals and dozens of churches, foundations, and organizations faithfully stand with us each year.

5. Attend an Immersion Night or an On-Site Educational Hour,

Come and see! Learn more about urban ministry and caring for the poor by going out on the streets under the guidance of Emmaus staff. An Immersion Night is appropriate for anyone over the age of eighteen and for groups of ten or more (individuals may join a previously scheduled group). On-Site Educational Hours provide an opportunity for groups to learn about the work of Emmaus and about urban ministry in general.

6. Organize a "Stories from the Streets" presentation, or have an Emmaus staff member speak at your church, school, or home.

Emmaus has two decades of experience in street ministry to those on the margins of our culture, and it is the only organization in the United States specifically dedicated to reaching out to men involved in street prostitution. We've developed "Stories from the Streets" to introduce the lives of these men to those who are unfamiliar with this issue. Through music, storytelling, and dramatic monologue, staff members Andi and Al Tauber (who are also singer/songwriters and worship leaders) encourage people to step out of their comfort zones and get involved in compassion-based ministry. "Stories from the Streets" has been performed on Moody Radio, at Focus on the Family, and at churches and colleges across the country.

7. Volunteer.

Give of your time regularly to reach out on the streets, work with our guys in the ministry center, or lend your talents and gifts to our administrative team in the office. Or, put together a group to come and do a day of service. Skills required: a love for Christ, a concern for the poor and broken, a kind heart, and a good listening ear.

8. Sponsor a food and clothing drive.

We're frequently looking for men's underwear, socks, and coats as well as toiletries such as razors, shaving cream, toothbrushes, and toothpaste. We're also always in need of canned goods, meat, and all kinds of food for our food pantry and for the daily meals we prepare for the men. People from around the country collect these items and ship them to us! Check out our Wish List to see what items we're currently in need of.

9. Participate in an Emmaus event and help promote it within your congregation or student body, and among your friends

Visit our website to learn about Emmaus events such as "The Endurance Ride," our annual bicycle fundraiser, and "Mercy in Motion," our spring arts benefit, and other events that help support our mission.

10. Join our Kaio Community or intern at Emmaus

Live in Christian community and volunteer full-time for one year to serve Emmaus and learn about urban ministry. A year in Kaio includes room and board, health insurance, a public transportation card, and a $20 per week stipend. Kaio is open to anyone eighteen years or older. Emmaus also hosts interns on a summer, semester, or shorter-term basis.

For more information on Emmaus or for any questions you might have, visit our website at www.streets.org, call 773-334-6063, e-mail emmaus@ streets.org, or write us at Emmaus Ministries, 921 W. Wilson Ave., Chicago IL 60640.

Appendix II

A Special Word about the Kaio Community

"They said to each other, 'Were not our hearts burning within us while he was talking to us on the road, while he was opening the scriptures to us?' (Luke 24:32)."

In the original Greek, Luke used the word *kaio*, which means "to set on fire." Ten years ago, echoing those two disciples as they walked the road to Emmaus burning with love for Jesus, we named an important aspect of our ministry the Kaio Community of Emmaus.

The name seemed more than appropriate since the men and women living in the Kaio Community are kindling the fire of God's love among guys they encounter on the streets of Chicago and bringing the lost to Christ.

* * * *

What would you do for fifty cents an hour?

I doubt if this was a question Ben was thinking as he listened to me speak about the work of Emmaus. I had been invited to St. John's Lutheran Church in rural Sidney, Ohio, by a childhood friend of mine who was the youth minister there at the time. I suspect that reaching out to urban male prostitutes is not a subject that piques the interest of most sixth-graders from Sidney, but Ben had paid attention and something I said stuck. Through his teen years, he would occasionally visit the Emmaus website and read a newsletter or two. He prayed for our guys, even though the individuals and their lives of prostitution on the streets of Chicago were unknown to him.

In Ben's sophomore year at the University of Colorado at Boulder, he spent his spring break working with a program called "Stand Up For Kids" in San Diego. "I spent a week hanging out with young homeless teenagers, many of whom were involved in prostitution," he said later. "For the first time, I put names and faces with those selling their bodies on the streets, and it broke my heart."

Returning to school, Ben finished his degree in environmental biology.

He considered teaching or working a job in the environmental field, but he couldn't ignore God's leading him to the city to work in street ministry. He visited the Emmaus website again and read about our Kaio Community.

Kaio members receive room and board, medical insurance, and a weekly stipend of twenty dollars (in other words, fifty cents an hour for a forty-hour week). In return, they're immersed in all aspects of the ministry.

Ben applied for Kaio and came for a visit. During his time with us, he knew that this was where God wanted him to be in the fall. So after spending the summer working in the Grand Tetons with young kids (sitting alongside riverbeds watching bison, elk and moose stroll by, and squinting up at soaring eagles), Ben arrived in Chicago to work with male prostitutes on the streets.

"There are definitely moments when I miss the peace and the beauty of the mountains," he says, "but I honestly feel blessed to be here and to have been given the chance walk alongside these men. A compassionate God asks us to go where there's hurt and to share the burden of one another's pain or brokenness or fear. At times that burden can be heavy, but it's a gift and a joy to get to know and care for these guys. It's a gift to see them become the men God created them to be."

Ben's initial commitment was for one year; he readily agreed to stay on for another. Besides doing outreach and working in our ministry center, Ben was the "Ride Master" for our Endurance Ride bicycle fundraiser.

* * * *

Katie heard me speak about Emmaus while she was a student at Wheaton College.

Initially, the idea of working with men involved in prostitution was intimidating to this suburban Chicago girl, but what intrigued her most was the opportunity to learn to live simply through our Kaio Community. Kaio members don't get paid much, but they have basic needs met, and live in the thick of ministry.

During her senior year in college she decided to volunteer with Emmaus as a way to "test it out." She found that she loved working with our guys. Outreach could be challenging, but she enjoyed talking with the men that dropped by the ministry center. Before graduation, she applied for, and was accepted into, the Kaio Community and worked full time in the center.

"Something Maurice mentioned at the dinner table last night really struck me," she says. "He said that during his time on the streets his family knew of his whereabouts. They knew what bars he frequented to pick up a 'date.' They knew where he bought drugs and got high. They knew what cheap hotels or shelters he stayed in, but never once did they come out and try and talk with him. But he always saw Emmaus teams in those areas. On the streets, in the bars, walking by crack houses and hotels, our presence was a reminder to him that God still cared. It reminded him that he was still worth something and that somebody still loved him."

Katie showed that Christlike love to our men everyday; her ever-present smile was a relief from the dreariness of the streets. After finishing her commitment as a Kaio member, Katie came on as a full-time, paid staff member. After several years on staff, she resigned to move on to her new job as a mom. Katie now serves as a member of the Emmaus board of directors.

* * * *

In this world of multimillion-dollar corporate salaries, billion-dollar defense budgets, and trillion-dollar deficits, it's amazing that someone would work for fifty cents an hour. But what Ben and Katie have learned and experienced at Emmaus this past year is worth more than any salary. And what we've gained from them is priceless.

What would you do for fifty cents an hour? Would you bring Good News to the poor? Sit and talk with the prodigal son in the distant country? Share your bread with the hungry? Visit the prisoner?

We have openings in our Kaio Community right now. Would you consider joining us? The salary is humble, but the benefits are eternal.

Appendix III

A Special Word about Immersion Nights

I faced the group I was addressing and watched their reactions to my words.

Bill looked like a deer frozen in the headlights of a car. He sat in front of me and listened to every word. His eyes were wide, his head unmoving, and it seemed he might bolt at any moment.

Janice sat on the couch to the right and appeared to oscillate through a range of emotions: fear, anticipation, excitement, then fear again. She held the arm of the sofa in a white-knuckled grip.

Fear.

It's a common emotion for those participating in an Emmaus Immersion Night. Bill and Janice are part of a young adult ministry from a suburban church near Chicago. They are in their late twenties, professionals, educated, well-off . . . and totally outside their comfort zones. A friend of theirs who's been volunteering with Emmaus for a couple years had invited them.

"Let me give you an idea of what you're going to be doing tonight., I said to Bill, Janice, and ten of their companions. "After our briefing here, we'll split your group into pairs and take the L [elevated train] down to the Lakeview neighborhood where we do our outreach. You and your partner will spend four hours walking the streets; meeting people; visiting clubs, bars and coffeehouses; and generally immersing yourselves in what we call the night community. Around midnight, your group will meet up at the Belmont L stop and come back here together for a debriefing."

Bill's eyes got even wider. I didn't think that was possible.

I continued with a description of the educational goals for the night, moved on to the practical aspects of Immersion Nights, and segued to a reassuring comment: "We have about six hundred people a year who attend these Immersion Nights. We only lost about five of them last year." *(Dramatic pause)* "Just kidding!" Nervous laughter rippled from couch to couch and equally nervous glances were exchanged. *Is he serious?*

The Immersion Night briefing lasts about an hour. I try to intersperse it with a lot of humor and stories about our ministry: our successes and failures, the good and the bad. In the end, I gather the group together for prayer, give them some passes for the L, and usher them out the door.

When Bill, Janice and others left they were still in the grip of a nervous state somewhere between fear and excitement.

For the next three or four hours, while I fiddled around the building or next door at my home, the Immersion Night group was out on the streets. They were talking with a homeless guy selling the "Streetwise" newspaper; sitting down in a twenty-four-hour Dunkin' Donuts with a homeless veteran; visiting gay bars like Gentry's and ordering a soft drink from a bartender who gives them a look that says, "Are you sure you know where you are?" They were hanging out in the Jewel supermarket on Broadway buying a young Jamaican guy with dreadlocks some food because he was begging; they were talking with a clerk in The Alley, a store advertised as an "alternative shopping experience" where everyone but them was dressed in black with multiple body piercings and spiked hair; they were standing on Halsted Street talking with a young hustler as he watched every passing car for the next trick.

Around midnight, when they met up at Belmont for the ride home, I was down in our ministry center putting some coffee on and making some hot chocolate. About 12:30 a.m. the front doorbell rang and I let the group in.

The fear they had carried with them walking out of the center was no longer there as they trooped back in. Only the excitement was left. I gave the group a few minutes to use the bathroom or get some coffee. Then we sat down for the debriefing.

"Tell me about some of your interactions."

Bill piped up right away; the deer-in-the-headlights gaze gone. "Debbie and I went to Gentry's. I didn't know what to make of the place. She got in a conversation with the bartender, and I turned to talk to the guy next to me. He asked what I was doing in a gay bar, and I said I was with a church from the suburbs who wanted to learn more about this community and came down for a night. He was pretty impressed with that. I introduced myself and he said cheerfully, 'I'm Robert, a gay Republican fundamentalist — everybody hates me!' We laughed together."

After Bill finished describing his conversation, I asked another person to share. Janice raised her hand and talked about sitting with Gerald in the

Dunkin' Donuts.

"He looked so lonely. I just introduced myself and we ended up talking with him for two hours! He is an amazing man. From how he looked it was pretty clear he was homeless, but he carried himself with a great sense of pride. He was smart, articulate, God-fearing, and a caring person." Janice continued for a while, tears welling up in her eyes when she described having to leave Gerald there when it was time to get back to the group.

After other people shared, I asked the group about their expectations. "What were you feeling as you left the ministry center earlier tonight?"

Fear was a common denominator.

"So where is that fear now?"

Gone.

"If it's gone, where did it come from in the first place and why?"

We had a great conversation.

I've found that when most people hear the terms "homeless," "prostitute," "addict" — or even "gay, Republican, fundamentalist" — they hear just the words, the concepts without names, without faces, without relationship. There's no connection with anything real or human.

The Immersion Night gives people an opportunity to put a name, a face and maybe a friend into the place of one of these nameless, faceless, relationship-less terms.

Getting to know people dispels our fears. It gives us an understanding that we can love these people and care for them as Jesus would. Christ doesn't call us to live our lives from positions of fear. That's not what this life is about.

Henry Ward Beecher was an American pastor in the mid-1800s who was a vocal abolitionist and one of the best preachers of his day. In his time, fear was rampant as slavery and war overshadowed the country. He, too, had a choice to live his life out of fear, but he chose a different course.

He once said, "God asks no man whether he will accept life. That is not the choice. You must take it. The only choice is how."

As people of faith we can't choose fear. We must choose courage.

Through our Immersion Night ministry, we're helping hundreds of Christians each year see how fear is a crippling factor in so much of our life and how Jesus continues to console, encourage, and command each of us to "be not afraid!"

With Much Thanks

I want to thank Dawn Herzog Jewell for coming alongside me and encouraging this book to get out of my head and onto print. I started writing "Streetwalking" in 2005. I find it easy to write about experiences I have with people on the street. What I don't find easy to do is to look internally at how and why those experiences are important to me. Dawn came alongside me for over a year and helped draw out those internal thoughts, insights, and reflections. Her constant pushing, encouragement, editing, and prayerful spirit did much to make this book a reality.

Thanks also to my friend Brian Bakke for providing the illustrations for this book. Brian is a husband, artist, and advocate for the poor. He works for the Mustard Seed Foundation, based in Washington, D.C., where he and his wife, Lisa, now live. For many years they lived in Uptown. In fact, it was to their apartment that Carolyn and I stopped by in Chapter Nine. I have always appreciated the way Brian captures urban life and people through his art, and I appreciate him doing these prints for "Streetwalking."

Last, thank you to all the staff, volunteers, and supporters who have made the mission of Emmaus Ministries a reality. I was able to mention a few of you throughout the book, but so many more have gone unnamed, for that I apologize. One co-worker whom I would like to thank in a special way is Christa Clumpner. She's served at Emmaus almost from the very beginning and is one of those "behind the scenes" people who really hate an acknowledgement like this, content to labor in quiet anonymity. Emmaus would not be the strong mission it is without all that she has given. Thank you, Christa.

I'd like to dedicate this book to my wife, Carolyn. It would be hard to imagine a more perfect companion for this journey.

Endnotes

1   MidAmerica changed its name to Good City in 2001 and is now under the leadership of Mike Ivers. This organization is among a growing number of leadership foundations that serve to support the work of faith-based individuals in urban environments.

2   This is from an article titled "Learned Helplessness," by Martin E. P. Seligman, Ph.D., Departments of Psychiatry and Psychology, University of Pennsylvania, Philadelphia, Pennsylvania. It can be found in Annual Review of Medicine, Vol. 23: 407-412. (The volume publication date is February 1972).

3   Fernandez-Alemany, Manuel (2000). "Comparative Studies on Male Sex Work in the Era of HIV/AIDS." The Journal of Sex Research. Vol. 37, 2: 187-190.

4   This is from a reading on the prophet Micah that InnerCHANGE uses in its formation of new missionaries. For more information on this ecumenical, missional order among the poor, visit www.innerchange.org.

5   Centers for Disease Control and Prevention, ACE Study: www.cdc.gov/ace/prevalence. htm.

6   Miller, R. L.; Klotz, D.; Eckholdt, H. (1998). "HIV Prevention with Male Prostitutes and Patrons of Hustler Bars: Replication of and HIV Preventative Intervention. American Journal of Community Psychology. Vol. 26, 1: 97-131.

7   The website of the National Association for Research and Therapy of Homosexuality has some excellent resources. One is an article by Bob Davies titled "Seven Things I Wish Pro-Gay People Would Admit," www.narth.com/docs/7things.html. For further reading, I'd also recommend "Ex-gays?" by Stanton Jones and Mark Yarhouse, and "Sexual Authenticity," by Melinda Selmys.

8   Archbishop Chaput was the keynote speaker at the 2002 fall banquet for Emmaus Ministries. His address, "Your Labor Is Not In Vain," is remarkable and can be read at www.streetwalkingwithjesus.com/files/chaput-2002.pdf.

9   Cates, J. A., & Markley, J. (1992). "Demographic, Clinical and Personality Variables Associated with Male Prostitution by Choice." Adolescence, Vol. 27, No. 107.

10 The UNAIDS organization reports that $15.8 billion dollars were allocated in 2008 alone for HIV prevention in the United States. See http://data.unaids.org/pub/Report/2009/ JC1796_Outlook_en.pdf.

11 "AIDS in America — Forgotten but Not Gone," Wafaa M. El-Sadr, M.D., M.P.H., Kenneth H. Mayer, M.D., and Sally L. Hodder, M.D. This article (10.1056/NEJMp1000069) was published on February 10, 2010, at NEJM.org.

12 *Evangelii Nuntiandi*, Pope Paul VI, December 8, 1975, No. 21.

13 Ibid., No. 22.

14 Wallace, Jim. *The Soul of Politics: Beyond "Religious Right" and "Secular Left"* (Mariner Books, 1995), p. 96.

15 Bureau of Justice Statistics, a component of the Office of Justice Programs in the U.S. Department of Justice. Summary of key facts: http://bjs.ojp.usdoj.gov/index.cfm?ty=kfa

16 Nouwen, Henri, *In The Name of Jesus: Reflections on Christian Leadership* (The Crossroad Publishing Company, 1992).

17 Scott, Michael, & Dedel, Kelly. (2006). "Problem-Oriented Guides for Police, Problem-Specific Guide Series." Street Prostitution, 2nd Ed. U.S. Dept. of Justice.

18 Permission for use of these lyrics was given by Peter Mayer on May 13, 2010, via e-mail.

19 Doherty, Catherine, Restoration newsletter, Vol. 26, No. 06, June 1973.

20 Newman, John Henry. *Meditations and Devotions of the Late Cardinal Newman* (Longmans, Green and Co., New York, 1907), p. 299.

21 Macready, Norra (1998). "HIV Prevention with Male Prostitutes and Patrons of Hustler Bars: Replication of an HIV Preventative Intervention." American Journal of Community Psychology. Vol. 26, 1: 97-131.

22 Day, Dorothy. *Loaves and Fishes* (Orbis Books, 1979), p. 79.

23 Allen, Donald M. (1980). "Young Male Prostitutes: A Psychosocial Study," Archives of Sexual Behavior, Volume 9, No. 5: 399-426.

24 Scott, Michael, & Dedel, Kelly (2006). "Problem-Oriented Guides for Police, Problem-Specific Guide Series." Street Prostitution, 2nd Ed., U.S. Dept. of Justice.

25 *Crack Pipe as Pimp* (1993). Mitchell S. Ratner (Ed.), Lexington Books, p. 86. An eighteenth-month study funded by National Institute on Drug Abuse.

26 Scott, Michael, & Dedel, Kelly (2006). "Problem-Oriented Guides for Police, Problem-Specific Guide Series." Street Prostitution 2nd Ed., U.S. Dept of Justice.

27 U.S. Department of Justice (2007). "On the Rights of Women and Children," Human Rights Record of the United States.

28 de Saint-Exupéry, Antoine, Citadelle (1948), translated into English as *The Wisdom of the Sands* (University of Chicago Press, 1984).